D0021331

THE LITTLE BOOK OF
Celtic
Names

Loreto Todd

THE O'BRIEN PRESS
DUBLIN

First published 2013 by The O'Brien Press Ltd.,
12 Terenure Road East, Rathgar, Dublin 6, Ireland
Tel: +353 1 4923333; Fax: +353 1 4922777
Material for this book was first published within a
longer text in *Celtic Names for Children*, Loreto Todd,
first published by The O'Brien Press 1998.
Copyright for text: Loreto Todd.
ISBN: 978-1-84717-329-4

British Library Cataloguing-in-publication Data
A catalogue record for this title is available from The British Library
1 2 3 4 5 6 7 8 9 10
13 14 15 16 17 18 19 20
Printed and bound in Poland by Białostockie Zakłady Graficzne S.A.
The paper in this book is produced using pulp from managed forests

The Celts

The Celts were once found all over Europe, from the Black Sea in the east to Ireland in the west, from south-west Spain and southern Italy through Switzerland and up as far north as Denmark. The Greeks called them Keltoi and evidence of their existence can be traced back to the fifth century BC. The Celts were known by different names in different areas: Galli or Gauls in France and parts of Italy, Galatae in the Balkans and Asia Minor, Celtiberi in Spain.

Apart from inscriptions found in various parts of Europe, most of our knowledge of the Celtic family of languages comes from what has become known as Insular Celtic, that is, the name given to the varieties found in Brittany and the British Isles.

Insular Celtic seems to have reached western Europe in two waves. The Goidelic (later Gaelic) Celts reached Ireland around the fourth century BC and this form of Celtic spread to the Isle of Man and Scotland. A second group, the Brythonic Celts, conquered and settled in parts of England, including Cornwall and Devon, and into Wales and Brittany. These groups spoke different varieties of Celtic.

The Celtic languages have all suffered serious decline, especially since the seventeenth century. The last mother-tongue speakers of Cornish died in the nineteenth century; the last mother-tongue speaker of Manx Gaelic in the 1970s. There are perhaps a million people who know some Breton but only a fraction of this number speak it fluently. Another two million speakers know Gaelic, in its Irish, Scottish and Cape Breton (Nova Scotian) forms, but perhaps only 200,000 speak it regularly and for most purposes. Welsh is probably the most vital of the Celtic languages, having as many as half a million regular users, including some speakers in Patagonia (Argentina) where 150 Welsh people settled in 1865.

Naming

Worldwide, naming has always been culturally significant and we often assume, incorrectly, that the system of first name(s) followed by a surname is universal. Surnames tend to be placed first in China and West Africa where, for example, Djou Dun Ren or Mbagwa Mary would be referred to in English as Mr Djou and Mrs Mbagwa. Surnames were not universal in the Celtic-speaking communities until the nineteenth century when Ap and Mac meaning 'son' were often used so that, in Wales, the son of Harry or Hugh might have become Ap + Harry

or Ap + Hugh, resulting in the blends Parry and Pugh. In Ireland, only the prefixes Mac (son) and Ó (descendant) are widespead, although the feminine form Ní, or Nic (daughter), is occasionally used as in Siubhan Ní Dhuibhir (daughter of Duibhir).

In choosing a child's first name, parents often say something about their hopes, their dreams, their aspirations. Sometimes, there is an association with God, as in the Hebrew Samuel (asked of God), or the Greek Dorothy (gift of God); often there is a link with love, as in the French-derived Amy (loved one), the Latin Alma (loving, kind), or the Lamso Bongcong (it is good to love). Parents have found inspiration, especially for their daughters, in nature – Daisy, Fern and Hyacinth; in jewels – Beryl, Jade and Pearl; in months of the year – Avril, April, May and June; and they have perhaps indulged in wishful thinking in the selection of virtues such as Constance, Felicity or Prudence. The spectrum of colours has provided Blanche (white), Rory (red) and Suneel (dark blue); places have given us Francis (man of France), Kirk (near the church) or Neville (new town); and aspects of warfare have provided a range of names, especially for sons, including Alexander (defender), Edgar (rich spear) and Finlay (fair-haired warrior).

Spelling and pronunciation

Many names have several spellings and a variety of pronunciations. The Irish forms of Catherine and John, for example, may occur as Caitlín, Caitlin, Caitríona, Cathleen, Kathleen; Caitlin may be pronounced as 'kotch+leen' or 'kot+leen' or 'koit+leen' or 'kate+leen' or 'kate+linn', and John as Seán, or Séan, Shaun, Shawn or Shane. And

these are the easy ones! Even within Ireland, there were several dialects, each with its own sound preferences, each with its own pet forms, some using a length mark or fada, others leaving the vowel unmarked. In addition, many of the names were recorded in Latin or French or English as well as Irish, thus providing a wide range of choice for parents and a nightmare for the dictionary maker. Some names have been adopted – and adapted – worldwide. Kevin, for example, has travelled widely from its origin as Caoimhín (beautiful birth) and was, for example, one of the ten most popular names for African American boys in 1982.

USING THIS BOOK

- **The book is divided into Girls' Names and Boys' Names.**
- **Names are entered in alphabetical order under the most frequently-used spelling.**
- **Variant spellings and versions are then listed according to popularity, thus not necessarily in alphabetical order.**
- **Some names may be listed under different letters, eg C and K, if commonly spelt with either initial letter.**
- **The most widely used pronunciations are given.**
- **A short history and/or interpretation of the name is given.**

5

Girls'
Names

Adaryn, Aderyn
('add+er+in')

This Welsh name comes from Welsh *aderyn*, meaning 'bird', and suggests a person who is not held back by earthly restrictions.

Aela *('ale+a')*

This Breton name is the feminine form of Ael and seems to be related to words for 'ardour' or 'rampart'.

Aelwen

This name can be Breton, Cornish or Welsh. It means 'fair of brow'. A broad brow was once associated with beauty.

Aerona, Aeronwen

Both of these names come from the Welsh *areon*, meaning 'berries'.

Africa, Africah, Aifric *('aff+rick')*

Records suggest that a twelfth-century queen of the Isle of Man was called Africa or Africah. This name was certainly inspired by the continent but probably reinforced by the Gaelic word *fioreach*, meaning 'noble'. The form Aifric is Gaelic and has been used in Scotland.

Aibhlínn, Eibhlínn *('I've+leen')*, Ava

It seems likely that the Normans took the name Aveline to Britain and Ireland. It developed several forms, including Aibhilín, Eveleen, Eveline, Evelyn and Evelyne. The name Aveline probably means 'longed-for child' and it may be the partial source of Ava.

Aibreán, Aibreann *('ab+rawn')*

This is the Gaelic form of the month 'April' and is sometimes used as a girl's name.

Aideen *('ay+deen')*

In Irish stories Aideen is related to Aedh and Aidan in its meaning of 'fire'. Aideen was the wife of Oscar, a grandson of Fionn Mac-Cool, and when Oscar was killed in battle she died of a broken heart.

Aileen, Ailene *('ay+leen')*

These are two of the many variants of Helen found in Ireland, Scotland and the Isle of Man. Helen comes from Greek *helios*, 'sun', and suggests 'sunbeam, ray of sunshine'.

Ailis, Ailish *('ale+ish' or 'isle+ish')*

This is the Irish form of a name brought to Ireland by the Normans as Alice and Alicia. The name is probably a variant of Adelaide, coming from Germanic *adal*, 'noble, well born' and *heid*, 'kind'.

Ailsa *('ale+sa')*

This Scottish name is probably derived from the island Ailsa Craig or 'rock island', which is in the Firth of Clyde.

Áine *('awe' + 'nia' like the ending of 'Sonia')*, Annie

Most people assume that this is an Irish form of Anne or Hannah, meaning 'God has favoured me', but it is, in fact, an old Irish name meaning 'brightness, luminosity' and could originally be used for either a male or a female. Áine may have been a fertility goddess. She was traditionally associated with generosity and Áines are supposed to be lucky in love and with money.

Ainslee, Ainsley, Ainslie

Ainsley was originally most frequently found in Scotland but is now popular elsewhere too. It is probable that the first syllable comes from Gaelic *aon*, meaning 'one', and that the second syllable may be from *laoi*, 'poem'.

Aislin, Aislinn, Aisling, Ashling *('ash+ling')*

Derives from the Gaelic word *aisling* 'dream, vision' and has become popular in Ireland, England and the USA. Its modern use is restricted to girls.

Alana, Alanna, Alannah *('al+an+na')*

This name derives from the Gaelic term of endearment *a leanbh* (child), although it is sometimes thought to be the feminine form of Alan and is found in all parts of the Celtic world.

Aleine *('a+lane')*

This form of Helen, meaning 'sunbeam', is sometimes written Eleyne. It was the name of Sir Gawain's niece. Aleine loved Sir Perceval and was instrumental in his becoming a Knight of the Round Table.

Almeda

This Breton name is becoming popular, especially for girls born in August. It is possible that it is a modified form of Latin *alma*, 'kind', influenced by *amanda*, 'worthy of love'.

Almha *('alva')*, Alva, Alvag

Almha was an Irish goddess renowned for her strength and prowess. The meaning of the name is not certain although it may be a form of *albha*, 'medication'. It seems to have been influenced by Latin *alma*, 'kind, nourishing'.

Amena, Amina, Amine

These variants are from a Celtic root meaning 'honest, utterly pure'. They are similar to the Arabic name Amena, meaning 'aspiration', and may also have been influenced by Amen, meaning 'so be it'.

Andrea, Andi

These are feminine forms of Greek Andreas (Andrew), meaning 'brave, manly, virile'. St Andrew is the patron saint of Scotland.

Aneira

Aneira is related to the Welsh noun *anrhydedd*, meaning 'honour'.

Angharad *('an+har+rid')*

This Welsh name is probably related to both *cariad*, 'love' and *cerydd*, 'reproach' and suggests 'without reproach'.

Anwen *('an+win')*

There are many Breton, Cornish and Welsh names that include a form of the adjective *gwen*, 'fair, white'. This one suggests 'very fair'.

Aobh, Aoibh *('eve' or 'ave')*

Aobh's name comes from Gaelic *aobh*, meaning 'beauty, radiance', and she was the first wife of King Lír and the mother of the four children who were turned into swans by Lír's second wife. The name is frequently equated with the biblical Eve, which probably comes from Hebrew *chava*, 'life'.

Aobhnaid, Aobhnait
('eve+nidge' or 'eve+nitch')

Aoibheann, Aoibhinn
('ay+von', 'eve+een' or 'eve+in')

This name is often interpreted as 'little Eve'. It comes, however, from Irish Gaelic *aoibhinn*, meaning 'of radiant beauty', and has a related form in Aobhnaid or Aobhnait. The name is sometimes anglicised as Eavan.

Aoibhel(l) *('ee+fell')*

This name comes from *aoibheall*, meaning 'joyful, beautiful'. Aoibhel was an Irish spirit woman who played the harp so beautifully that anyone who heard the music died from utter joy.

Aoife *('eef+a')*

Aoife is related to Aoibheann. It means 'radiance, joy' and is often used as the Irish equivalent of 'Eve', which probably comes from the Hebrew *chava*, meaning 'life'.

Arlen, Arlena, Arlene, Arlène

These Breton names are probably derived from the French place Arles, although they may also derive from Celtic words meaning 'binding promise after consultation'. The name is found in France as Arlène.

Armelle

It seems likely that Armelle comes from Brittany, where it is said to mean 'high ranking lady; princess'. There are many possible Celtic source words for this name. Gaelic, for example, has *áirmeach*, 'famous, splendid'.

Athracht, Attracta
('a+troct' or 'a+track+ta')

Many people have assumed that Attracta comes from the Latin verb *attrahere*, meaning 'draw towards, attract', and it is likely that this meaning has contributed to its use. A form occurs, however, in sixth-century Ireland as that of one of a number of female saints who gave up a life of comparative luxury for one of dedication. Athracht may, therefore come from a Gaelic noun *athrach*, 'change, alteration'.

Aude *('aud' or 'ode')*

The name Aude occurs both in Brittany and in Cornwall, where a saint of this name was beheaded in the tenth or eleventh century. It is uncertain what Aude means but it seems to be related to the name Gunoda and thus to mean 'blessed'.

Awena

This Welsh name comes from *awen*,

'muse', and suggests 'poetic, inspirer of poetry'.

B

Baibín *('bah+been')*, Bairbín, Báirbre *('bar+breh')*, Barba, Barbara, Barbra

The Greek word *barbara* meant 'foreign woman' and it was adopted into Latin as a woman's name, Barbara. The Celts adopted it because of the popularity of the legend of St Barbara. She was executed by her father because she refused to give up her attachment to Christianity. He was punished by being struck by a bolt of lightning.

Banba, Banbha
('ban+bah', 'ban+vah')

Banba is believed to have been one of the first settlers in Ireland. It is not clear what her name means but it is associated with *bean*, meaning 'woman' and so has similar implications to the biblical 'Eve'. There is a legend about Ireland having been at one time a country inhabited only by women, Tír na mBan, with Banba as their queen.

Béibhinn *('bay+veen')* Bevan, Bevin, Vivanne, Vivian, Vivien, Vivienne

This name is almost certainly a blend of *bean*, 'woman', and *finn* or *fionn* 'fair', and the term may originally have been applied to Viking women. Because the vocative form of Béibhinn would be pronounced 'Vayveen', the name was associated with the Norman Vivian, meaning 'alive, living'.

Beriana, Bberion, Buryan

This Cornish name is found in a variety of forms. Her name may mean 'gift' and so be related to Gaelic *beir*. Beriana is reputed to have cured a prince who was paralysed.

Bethan, Betha, Beatha
('ba+ha')

There are three possible sources for these names. They may be a blend of (Eliza)beth + Anne, Hebrew names meaning 'God is my oath' and 'God has favoured me'. They may possibly be a reduction of the Hebrew Bethany, meaning 'house of dates' and reputed to be the place where Mary, Martha and Lazarus lived (Luke, 19: 29). They may also be from the Gaelic word *beatha*, meaning 'life'. The name of the Scottish king Macbeth certainly means 'son of life'.

Betrys

This Welsh form of Beatrice would have appealed to many Celts, who would have known the story of Saint Beatrix. She was probably originally called 'Viatrix', 'voyager through life', but her name was modified after she was persecuted in Rome in the fourth century: Beata Viatrix, 'Blessed Viatrix', gave way to Beatrix and Beatrice.

Blaine, Blayne

Blaine is probably from a Gaelic word *bléan* meaning 'narrow, hollow'. It may also mean 'white, fair' and come from *bléin-fhinne*, 'whiteness'.

Bláithín *('blah+heen')*
Blaithnéid *('blaw+nade')*
Bláthnaid *('blaw+nid)*
Blathnait *('blaw+nit')*
Blanaid *('blaw+nidge')*

These names are all variants of the Gaelic noun *bláth*, meaning 'flower'. Bláthnaid fell in love with Cúchulainn and helped him to defeat her husband so that they would be free to marry.

Blodwen

Blodwen is a compound of Welsh *blodyn*, meaning 'flower', and *gwyn*, meaning 'white, holy'.

Bonnie, Bonny

In Scotland and parts of Northern Ireland, the adjective 'bonnie', which derives from French *bon*, *bonne*, 'good', means 'pretty, attractive'. It is sometimes used as a name, partly perhaps as a result of the popularity of Margaret Mitchell's novel *Gone with the Wind*: the nickname of Scarlett O'Hara's daughter was Bonnie.

Branna, Brannagh

('bran+na')

Branna may be the female equivalent of Celtic *bran*, meaning 'raven' and found in some form in all of the Celtic-using communities. It may also be a variant pronunciation of Brenna or a derived form of the surname Brannagh.

Bree, Breeanne, Brianne *('bree+anne')*

This name may be related to Bríd, who was a Celtic goddess whose name, in the form of *brighid*, came to mean 'beautiful maiden'. The form Breeanne may be a blend of Bree and Anne or a feminine form of Brian, meaning 'eminence'.

Brenda

Until this century, Brenda was virtually unknown outside Scotland. It is often taken to be the female form of Brendan, a name that may come from Welsh *brenhinol*, meaning 'royal'; it is also possible that it is a modified form of the Viking word *brand*, meaning 'bright sword'.

Brenna

It is not easy to say whether Brenna is a form of Brenda, or a female form of Bran, or a form of Brynna, a female form of Welsh *bryn*, meaning 'hill'. It has been suggested that Brenna, from Irish *breana*, is a name in its own right meaning 'beauty with hair as dark as a raven'.

Briallen

Briallen is a Welsh floral name. It is taken over from *briallen*, the word for 'primrose'.

Briana *('bree+an+na')*, Bryana, Bryna

These are feminine forms of Brian and mean 'noble, virtuous'.

Bríd *('breej')*
Bride, Bridie, Brídín *('bree+jean')*, Bregeen, Bridget, Bridgeteen, Brighid, Brigid, Brigit, Brigiteen, Brigitte, Bree, Breda, Breege, Berc'hed, Biddie, Biddy, Birgitta

It seems likely that Bríd was a Celtic goddess, possibly of agriculture and healing, possibly of poetry and fire, and sometimes known as 'Brigid of the Holy Fire'. Her name is related to the noun *brígh*, meaning 'power, strength, vigour, virtue'. Many of the attributes of the goddess were applied to St Brigid of Kildare who died during the first quarter of the sixth century and who is reputed to be buried in Downpatrick, in the same grave as St Patrick and St Colmcille. St Brigid was often referred to as the 'Mary of the Gael' and her feast day on 1 February coincides with the Feast of Candles, itself possibly a relic of the celebration of the victory of light over darkness.

Brittany, Brittney

It is not unusual for placenames to be given to daughters. Brittany is the English name for the part of France that the Bretons call Breiz and the French call Bretagne.

Brona ('bro+nah'), Brónagh, Brónach ('bro+nock')

The Gaelic adjective *brónach* means 'sad, sorrowful' and could, at one stage, be used as a name for either a girl or a boy.

Brongwyn ('brong+win'), Bronwen, Bronwyn, Brangwyn, Branwen

This Welsh name, which occurs in a variety of forms, derives from *bron* + *gwen*, meaning 'breast' + 'fair, pure, white' and was once given as a mark of respect to someone who was either physically or spiritually beautiful.

Brynna, Bryony

It is not certain where these names originated. Brynna may be a feminine form of Welsh Bryn, meaning 'hill', and Bryony may be a variant of this, possibly influenced by the name of the plant *brionia*.

C

Caera ('care+a'), Ceara

Caera seems to come from a Gaelic word *cearbh*, meaning 'sharp, spear-like', 'desire'. This may not sound particularly appropriate for a little girl, but 'spear' could mean 'in a direct line on the father's side'. In addition, it is similar in form to Cara, meaning 'friend, loved one'.

Cairenn ('care+in'), Caryn, Karen, Karin, Karel, Keren

Cairenn was the mother of the legendary Niall of the Nine Hostages and the concubine of King Eochu. Her name seems to come from Irish *cara* + *-ín*, meaning 'little beloved' and, although it may be pronounced like Karen or Karin, it is not a borrowing from the Viking languages or an Irish form of Katherine. The name Karen and a variant Karel are found in Brittany.

Caitlín *('kotch+leen' or 'koit+leen', but 'kate+lynn' in America)* **Caitlin, Cathleen, Cathline, Katelin, Kaytlin, Kaytline, Kaytlyn**

This name occurs in a variety of variants, as well as the abbreviated forms Cait, Cayt, Cass and Cassie. It is probable that all of these and the variants that are formed around Caitríona are borrowed via Latin from the Greek *Aikaterinë*, the name of a young woman martyred in Alexandria in the early years of the fourth century. St Catherine's name came to be associated with courage and purity, qualities that were attractive to the Celts.

Caitríona, Catriona
('cat+tree+on+a')

Caitríona is popular in Ireland, Scotland and the Isle of Man. Like Kathleen, it may be a borrowing from Greek *Aikaterinë* and is thought to mean 'clear, pure'.

Camryn

The spelling looks Welsh but this name is often a female form of Cameron – *cam shrón* (meaning 'crooked nose'!).

Caoilfhinn *('kay+lin')*, Kaylin, Kaylynn, Keelan, Keelin

Caoilfhinn comes directly from Irish *caoil fhinn*, meaning 'slender and fair' and implying 'very beautiful'.

Caoimhe, Keeva, Keva

There are two explanations for this name and they are both probably correct. The name may come directly from Irish *caoimhe*, 'gentleness, beauty, grace, courtesy', or it may be a feminine form of the male name Caoimhín.

Cara, Caragh *('car+ah')*

Cara is the Irish word for 'friend'. It is possible that it was originally borrowed from Latin. Indeed, *cara* in Italian means 'beloved'.

Carol, Caryl, Caryll, Carys

The name Carol is often a form of Latin *Carolus*, meaning 'Charles', reinforced by the word 'carol' meaning a Christmas hymn. However, the Irish name Cearbhall or Cearúl, probably meaning 'courageous in war', was anglicised as Car(r)ol(l) and so may have contributed to the popularity of the name. The Welsh *cariad*, meaning 'beloved', has helped to popularise Caryl and Carys in Wales.

Caronwyn *('car+on+in')*

This Welsh name comes from *car* + *gwyn* and means 'love + fair', implying 'beautiful loved one'. It is possible that it was influenced by French Cheron, or Caron, also meaning 'beloved, dear one'.

Ceinlys *('cane+liss')*

This Welsh name may be a blend of *tlws*, 'gems' + *melys*, 'sweet', and so imply beauty, wealth and sweetness of character.

Ceiridwen, Ceridwen *('care+id+win')*

This Welsh name is probably a blend of *cerdd*, 'poetry' + *gwen*, 'pure, fair, white'. An early Ceridwen was the goddess of poetry and was married to Tegid Foel.

Ceri, Cerian, Kerry

Ceri is popular in Wales and Cornwall and is sometimes used as a spelling for Kerry. It is not certain whether it is a shortened form of Ceridwen, meaning 'beautiful as a poem' or whether it is from the Welsh *car*, which is the equivalent of Irish *cara*, 'friend'.

Ciara, Ciarra, Keera, Keira, Keyra, Kiera, Kira, Kyara ('key're+a')

Ciara is a feminine form of Ciaran and comes from Irish *ciar*, meaning 'dark brown'.

Clíodhna ('klee+en+a'), Cliona, Cleona

The meaning of this Irish name is uncertain, although it may be related to *clódhna*, 'exceptionally thin' or *cliath*, the word for a system of musical notation, and this latter would be appropriate as Clíodhna is sometimes described as a poetic muse.

Clodagh ('clo+da')

It seems likely that Clodagh or Clóda has been taken over from the Clóideach, the name of a river in Tipperary, Ireland. In this it resembles Shannon.

Colleen, Colene, Coleen

This name comes from the Gaelic word *cailín*, meaning 'girl'. It was used by people of Irish descent in America, Australia and South Africa.

Columba, Koulm, Koulmia

As well as the Irish male saint Columba, there was a fourth-century Cornish female saint of the same name, coming from Latin *columba*, meaning 'dove'.

Cora, Coralie, Corey, Cori, Kori

The name Cora and the French Coralie both seem to derive from a Greek word *korë*, meaning 'maiden'. In this sense, they parallel Colleen. Cora and Córa, are used in parts of Ireland as a feminine form of Corey, which is a common surname and probably a form of the Germanic name Godfrey, from *god + frid*, meaning 'the peace of God'.

Crystal, Kristell, Krystell

Crystal is an example of the popularity of gemstones as the name for a girl. This one comes from Greek *krystallos*, 'ice', but it has been reinforced in Celtic communities by the existence of the surname 'McCrystal', by the Celtic words for 'Christian', and by the medieval legend of Crystabel(l). The name Krystell is found in Brittany.

Crystyn

This is a modern Welsh form of Christine. It can mean 'crust', but the usual meaning is 'follower of Christ'.

D

Dacey, Dacie

Although the link is not immediately apparent, this name is related to Desmond as they both use the Gaelic *deas*, meaning 'south', so Dacey means 'southern girl'.

Daimhín *('daw+veen')*, Davina

These names are thought to be from the same source but they seem to have arisen separately in Ireland and Scotland. *Daimhín* means 'little deer' and it has produced the surnames Davane and Devine. Davina is used in Scotland as a feminine form of David, but the Celtic influence from *daimhín* may have contributed to its popularity.

Daireann *('dar+rawn')*, Darran

This name probably comes from *dáir* and means 'fruitful, bountiful', although it may also be related to *dair*, 'oak tree'. One of the earliest references we have to Daireann is to a beautiful young woman who fell in love with Fionn MacCool

and wanted him as her husband –
for a year.

Dana, Danu, Dayna

This is one of the oldest names
in the Celtic tradition. Dana or
Danu or Anu seems to have been
a mother god, revered in Indo-
European traditions from India to
Ireland. It is not certain what her
name means but it is associated
with power and generosity. In Ireland, it is further reinforced by the
Gaelic words *dán*, meaning 'poem',
and *dána*, meaning 'brave, daring'.

Dara, Deri

Dara is a Gaelic name coming
from *dair* meaning 'oak' and is
related to the word *doire*, meaning 'oak grove'. The name may be
either male or female, but there
is a tendency for Dara and Deri
to refer to girls, and Darach and
Derry to be reserved for boys.

Darfhinn *('dar+rin')*, Dairinn, Dareena, Darena, Darina, Daron

This name may well be a modified
form of Dara with the diminutive
ending -*ín*. The modern spellings
have probably been influenced by
Doreen, which means 'gift'. Dar-
fhinn or Dairinn seems to mean
'daughter of Finn' or possibly
'golden-haired daughter', where
'*finn*' is the adjective 'fair'.

Dearbhail, Dearbhal *('jar+ville')*, Deirbhile *('jar+villa' or 'jer+villa')*, Dervla

The name Dearbhail seems to be
related to *dearbha*, meaning 'genu-
ineness' and Deirbhile may be
deirbh + file, meaning 'daughter or
relative of the poet', but they have
both contributed to Dervla, and so
are treated under the same heading.

Dearbhorgaill

('der+vor+gill'), **Devorgilla**

This name may be a development from Dearbhail or it may be *deirbh + Forgall* and mean 'daughter or relative of Forgall'. There are at least two Devorgillas in Irish literary tradition. The first was in love with Cúchulainn and was angry when he rejected her. However, they settled their differences and became as close as brother and sister. The second was a twelfth-century queen who ran away from her husband to live with Diarmuid, the man she loved.

Deirdre *('dear+dree' or 'dare+drih')*, **Deirdriú, Deidre**

The meaning of Deirdre is not certain although it may be related to *deireadh*, meaning 'end'. Her love story is one of the most beautiful in Irish literature. She was betrothed to King Conchubhar but was in love with Naoise, one of the sons of Usna. Deirdre and Naoise ran away to Scotland with Naoise's brothers. They were tricked into returning to Ireland where Naoise was killed. Deirdre threw herself from a chariot rather than live without the man she loved.

Delia, Dilic, Dilecq, Dilecta, Dilie, Dillie, Dilys *('dill+iss')*

Dilie and Dillie occurred in Ireland as forms of Delia, a Greek name meaning 'from Delos', and this usage may have been reinforced by the Irish adjective *dílis*, 'genuine, proper'. Forms of this name occur in Brittany, Cornwall, Ireland and Wales, and they may have nothing in common but their similarity of form. It is possible that there were two Cornish saints, one Dilic and one Dilie. The form Dilecq seems to have been used in Brittany as well as the Latinised form Dilecta, which relates to 'beloved'. Welsh Dilys seems to have come from the adjective *dilys*, 'genuine'.

Delwyn, Delwin

There are many Welsh names beginning with Del-, all related to *del* implying 'pretty'. Delwyn suggests both 'pretty' and 'fair'.

Derryth *('der+rith')*, Derry, Deri

This particular name is Welsh and is related to *derw*, 'oaken', and *derwydd*, 'druid'. The name is close in form and meaning to Gaelic *doire*, meaning 'oak grove'.

Devin, Devon

Both these names have been inspired by the English county, whose Celtic name seems to mean 'deep valley'. They could also have been influenced by Welsh *dewin*, 'magician', and Gaelic *dán*, 'gift'.

Don

Don was the oldest Welsh mother god and is, therefore, in some ways, equivalent to Irish Dana. She is associated with water and her name is found in such rivers as the Danube in Europe and the Don in Yorkshire. She was thought to have taken up her home in the skies and the constellation Cassiopeia was called *Llys Don*, 'Don's Court'.

Donalda

Donalda is the female form of Scottish Donald, which comes from Scots Gaelic Domhnul and means 'ruler of the world'.

Dorian, Dorien

Oscar Wilde seems to have created the name Dorian for the title character in *The Picture of Dorian Gray*. The name has been transferred to girls partly because of its similarity to Dora, Doreen and Doris, but Wilde may also have been influenced by the Irish name *Dairinn*, which meant 'daughter of Fionn MacCool'.

Dymphna *('dimf+na')*, Dimpna, Dympna, Damhnaid *('dav+nid')*, Damhnait *('dow+nid')*

It is possible that Dymphna and Damhnaid are two different Irish names, both of which are related to *dán*, 'poetry'. St Dymphna was the seventh-century daughter of an Irish king. According to legend, she fled to Belgium in order to become a nun. She is buried near Antwerp.

E

Eamair, Eimear, Emer *('aim+er' or 'eem+er')*

Cúchulainn's wife's name is most frequently represented as Emer. It is not certain what the name means, although it may be related to *eamhean*, 'twin'.

Eavan, Aoibhinn

Eavan is an anglicisation of the Irish *aoibhinn*, meaning 'attractive, beautiful, radiant'.

Edana, Edna

Edana and Edna are almost certainly anglicised forms of Eithne, which comes from Irish *eithne*, 'nut kernel', or *aodh*, meaning 'fire'.

Éibhleann, Eibhlín *('ayve+linn' or 'eve+linn')*, Eileen, Elaine

Éibhleann is a Gaelic word, related to *aoibhinn*, meaning 'radiance' and it probably combined with biblical Eve, meaning 'life', and Norman Aveline and Elaine, 'like the sun', to provide of the above names and their derivatives. The name Eileen is closely associated with Ireland and has featured in songs, poetry and plays such as 'Eileen McManus' or 'Eileen a Rún', often symbolising the young woman who had to emigrate to help support her family.

Éilis, Eibhlís
('eye+lish' or 'ail+ish')

These names were probably borrowed into Irish from the Norman Alice, meaning 'noble', and reinforced by the Hebrew Elizabeth, meaning 'God is my oath'.

Eilwen *('al+win')*

Eilwen is from Welsh *æl + gwyn*, meaning 'fair brow', a phrase that is equivalent to 'beautiful'.

Éire *('air + rih')*, Erin, Erina, Eriu

Éire was a goddess who lived with her sisters Banba and Fódla in Ireland. Each of the three sisters wanted the country to be called after her, so they held a race. By a mixture of talent and guile, Éire won. In due course, the country became Éire and later Éire + land:

Ireland. Erin is a modified form of Éire. The form Erina suggests 'Irish girl' and has been influenced in form by Erena, meaning 'peace'.

Eireen *('i+reen')*, Éireann *('air+in')*

Eireen is possibly a blend of Irene, from Greek *eirene*, meaning 'peace', and Éire, meaning 'Ireland'. Éireann is either a variant of Éire or a blend of Éire and Ann.

Eirwen

If Snow White had been given a Welsh name, she would have been called Eirwen, because *eira* means 'snow' and *gwyn* is 'white' or 'fair'.

Eithna *('eth+na')*, Eithne, Ethniu

These names may all come from Irish *eithne*, 'nut kernel', or be related to Aodh or Aidan and thus mean 'fire, little fire'. Eithne was a goddess, and there are also several saints called Eithne. According to tradition, she lived on milk alone as a means of purifying her body.

Elen

Elen is a Welsh form of Helen, which comes from Greek *helios*, 'sun' and means 'like the sun, sunbeam, radiant'.

Elspeth

Elspeth is a Scottish form of Elizabeth, which is a Hebrew name meaning 'God is my oath'.

Ena

Ena is sometimes regarded as a pet form of Eithne and so means 'little fire'. It has also been used as an abbreviation for Eugenia, from Greek *eugenios*, meaning 'nobly born'.

Enda, Eneda

Enda derives from Gaelic *éan*, meaning 'bird', and suggests freedom of spirit. The sixth-century St Enda was a monk and there is also a Cornish female saint called Eneda. The name is used for boys and girls.

Enid, Enida

Enid probably comes from Welsh *enaid*, meaning 'soul' and suggesting 'purity of soul'.

Enya

Enya may come from *eithne*, 'nut kernel', or may mean 'flame'. It may have started as a form of Eithne or Áine, meaning 'brightness'.

Etain, Étáin *('ey+taw+in' or 'ee+taw+in')*, Eadain

This name may play on the Gaelic word *éad*, meaning 'jealousy'. It also occurs in several other forms, including Édaín and Éadaoin.

Eurwen

This Welsh name combines *aur*,

'gold' and *gwyn* 'fair' and may thus be taken as the equivalent of 'beautiful, golden girl'.

F

Fainche *('fan+che' or 'fan+ke' or 'fine+che')*

Although this Irish name looks remarkably similar to the Breton form of Francis, it is unrelated. The name may be related to *faing*, 'raven', or *fáineóir*, 'wanderer'. One of the saints to bear this name was the sister of Saint Enda.

Fanch, Franseza, Soaz

Fanch is the Breton equivalent of Francis and the name is occasionally used for a girl, although the forms Franseza and Soaz are preferred. Like all forms of Francis, Fanch means 'from France' and it was originally a nickname.

Fay

This name may have originated in France, where *foi* used to be pronounced like 'fway' and meant 'faith'. It was, however, absorbed into Irish culture where a person may still be described as 'fay', meaning 'having mystical powers' or 'fated'. It is thought by some to be a short form of Faith and is thus linked to 'fidelity'.

Fedelma, Fidelma

This traditional Gaelic name goes back at least 1,500 years and has been held by saint and warrior. Its Celtic meaning is not certain although it may be linked to *feidhle*, meaning 'constancy'. It closely resembles Latin names, such as Fidelia, 'the faithful one'.

Fflur

Fflur is a Welsh name, meaning 'flower' and roughly equivalent to Blodwyn. It seems to have been borrowed from French *Fleur*.

Fiona, Ffion, Ffiona

Fiona is extremely popular throughout the British Isles but is mostly associated with Scotland. Fiona has two possible sources. One is from Latin *vinum*, 'wine', which is *fíon* in modern Irish. The second is from *f(i)on(n)*, meaning 'fair, white, beautiful'. Ffion is occasionally used in Wales and is a Welsh spelling of Fiona.

Fionnuala, Fionola, Finola, Fenella, Nuala

One of the most beautiful stories in Irish Celtic mythology centres on Fionnuala, whose name comes from *fionnghuala* and means 'fair shoulders'. According to legend, King Lír and his wife Aobh had a daughter, Fionnuala, and three sons, Aedh, Conn and Fiachra. When Aobh died, Lír's new wife, Aoife, was jealous of her husband's love for his children and bribed a sorcerer to kill them. The sorcerer could not take away the lives of such pure children and so transformed them into swans.

Flanna

Flanna is the female form of Flann and so means 'bright red'. Many people find it attractive because it includes Anna, a name that means 'full of grace'.

Frann

Frann is a name that suggests freedom and may come from *fraochán*, 'sea bird'.

G

Gael, Gaelle, Gail, Gayle *('gale')*

Gael, or *gaedheal*, is occasionally used in Celtic communities as the name of a Gaelic-speaker or a person who is from Ireland, Scotland or the Isle of Man. The selection of Gael as a girl's name has been influenced by the abbreviated form of Abigail, a Hebrew name that means 'Father of Exaltation'.

Gaynor

Gaynor is probably an anglicised form of Guinevere, which comes from Welsh *gwyn*, 'white, pure' + *hwyfar*, 'smooth', and means 'fair and beautiful'.

Gilda

Gilda is a Gaelic name from *giolla* + *Dia*, meaning 'servant of God'. 'Gil-' was often used in Irish and Scottish communities to mean people who devoted themselves to another, and so we get Gilchrist, 'the servant of Christ'. The adjective *gile* means 'brightness, whiteness, the purest of the pure' and so the name could also mean 'the perfection of God'.

Gladys *('glad+iss')*, Gladez, Gwladus, Gladuse

Gladys is an anglicised form of Welsh *gwladys*, meaning 'delicate flower', or possibly being a Welsh form of Latin *Claudia*. The name was popular in Brittany, where it occurs as Gladez, and in Cornwall where St Gwladus(e) was a popular saint.

Glenda, Glenna

These Welsh variants probably come from Welsh *glan*, 'clean', + *da*, 'good', and imply 'purity'; or they may be from *glyn*, 'valley', and mean 'girl from the valley'.

Glenys, Glynis, Glynys *('glen+iss' or 'glin+iss')*

Glenys may be a blend of Glenda and Gladys, or it may be a form of Glynis, from Welsh *glyn*, 'valley', and meaning 'valley girl'.

Gobhnet, Gobnaid *('gub+nidge')*, Gobnait *('gub+nit')*

Gobnait's name is often given as

the Irish equivalent of Barbara, which means 'foreign woman'. It is also possible that the first part of the name comes from Irish *gob*, meaning 'mouth', and may have been applied to one who was skilled with words. A fifth-century nun of this name built her chapel in Ballyvourney, County Cork.

Gráinne, Grania
('graw+nya' or 'gra+in+nyih)

Gráinne's name may be derived from Irish *gráidhte* and so mean 'the loved one', or it may mean 'grain of corn', thus linking her with an earlier goddess of the harvest. She was the daughter of Cormac Mac Art and had been promised in marriage to the king, Fionn Mac-Cool. When Gráinne saw him at the wedding feast, she knew he was too old for her. She fell in love instead with Fionn's nephew, Diarmuid, and she encouraged him to run away with her. Their punishment was a curse that prevented them spending two consecutive nights in the same place.

Guinevere *('gwin+a+vere')*, Gwenhwyfar, Jennifer, Jenniver

Guinevere is perhaps the best-known heroine in Celtic literature. Her name comes from *gwen + hwyfar*, 'fair + smooth', and means 'the fair one'. According to legend, she was the most beautiful woman on earth. She was married to King Arthur but she fell in love with Lancelot and, because of their adultery, the peace of Camelot was shattered. The name was at one time so popular that it had a Cornish form, Jenniver/Jennifer, which developed into a name in its own right.

Gwen, Wenn

Cornwall had St Gwen, who was also referred to as Wenn. The name is probably the equivalent of

Welsh *gwyn*, meaning 'white, pure, holy'.

Gwendolen, Gwendolena, Gwendolina, Gwendoline, Gwendolyn

These variants probably come from *gwyn*, 'holy, white', + *dolen*, 'ring', and the name has been popular in Wales, Cornwall and Brittany, where the forms ending in '-a' are preferred. One of the earliest records of the name refers to Gwendolena, Merlin's wife.

Gwyneth ('gwin+ith')

Gwyneth may be a form of Welsh *gwynaeth*, 'luck', or, if it comes from *gwendydd*, it may mean 'bliss'.

Gwynne ('gwin' or 'gwen'), Gwenn, Gwyn, Gwynn, Gwen, Gwenne,

Gwenna, Gwennaig, Winifred, Wynne

Gwynne comes from Welsh *gwyn*, meaning 'fair, white, pure, blessed'. It is more frequently used for a boy than for a girl. Gwenn is preferred in Brittany and it also occurs there as Gwenna and Gwennaig.

H

Haley, Hayley

This name, popularised by the actress Hayley Mills, may come from Old English and mean 'hay field', or Gaelic *éalaigh*, 'escape'.

Haude ('ode')

Haude is a Breton name, probably derived from Ada or Adèle and meaning 'noble'.

Heulwen, Heulwyn ('hyool+win' or 'hool+wen')

Heulwen comes from Welsh *heulwen*, meaning 'sunshine'.

Íde ('eed+deh'), Ida, Ita, Ite

Íde is from the Irish word *íde*, meaning 'thirst (for goodness and knowledge)' and, as one might expect, it was the name of a saint closely associated with education. The forms Ita and Ite are also used.

Imogen, Inogen
('im+o+gin', 'in+o+gin')

It seems probable that Inogen comes from Gaelic *inghean* or *inighion*, meaning 'daughter'. The form with '-m-' may have been influenced by 'image'.

Ineda ('een+ay+da')

Ineda was a Cornish saint, sometimes called Eneda. This name may be from Gaelic *eithne*, 'kernel', or may be related to *aodh*, 'fire, flame'.

Inira, Inire, Ynyra
('in+eer+a')

These Welsh names mean 'honour' and are the equivalent of Honoria.

Iona ('eye+o+na'), Ione

Iona is the name of a Scottish island that has been adopted for girls. Its meaning is uncertain but its association with religion makes the name the equivalent of 'blessed'.

Iseabeal ('ish+a+bale'), Iseabeul, Sibéal, Shibley

These names are based on Isabel, the Spanish form of Elizabeth. All the European versions of the name of John the Baptist's mother come from a Hebrew name, *Elisheba*, meaning 'God is my oath'. The Irish ending *-béal* and the Scottish ending *-beul* suggest a link with 'mouth' that does not, in fact, exist.

Iseult ('ee+solt'), Isolde, Isolt, Essyllt, Yseult

These names are probably all derived from Welsh *Esyllt*, a name that means 'the beautiful one'.

There are several Iseults in literature but the most famous is Iseult of Ireland, the wife of Mark of Cornwall who fell in love with Tristan, her husband's nephew. They became lovers, but Mark banished Tristan to Brittany.

J

The letter 'j' was not used in the early Celtic alphabets, and so only a few Celtic names begin with it.

Jocelyn *('joss+el+linn')*

Jocelyn was originally a boy's name, but it is now used for a girl. It may come from an old German name meaning 'connected with the Goths' and it seems to have been used by the Normans in the form Joscelin, or it may be a diminutive of Joyce, from Judocus, a Latinised form of *iod*, 'lord'.

Joyce

It has often been suggested that Joyce comes from Old French *joir*,

'to be joyous, happy', but it is more probable that it comes from the seventh-century Breton hermit and saint, Judoc.

K

Kacee, Kaci, Kasey *('kay+see')*

These are variants of Gaelic *cathasach*, 'vigilant, alert in war'. They are modern forms of Casey.

Kaitlin, Kaitlyn, Kaytlin, Kaytlyn

These are recent spellings of Caitlin, a form of Catherine, which is related to Greek *katharos*, 'pure'. They are almost exclusively American and are usually pronounced like 'Kate+Lynn'.

Karel

Karel is a Breton name, related to Carol, from Carola, a female form of Charles, which probably comes from a Germanic *carl*, meaning 'man' or 'strong'. The Breton form may have been influenced by the Irish surname 'Carroll', which may come from *cearbh*, 'elk' .

Katell

Katell is a Breton form of the Greek-inspired name Catherine, from *katharos*, 'pure, clear'. The Celts all seem to have used a form with 'l' as well as a form with 'r', and so we have both Caitlín and Caitriona.

Kathleen

Kathleen has been used so often for Irish girls that it has become almost a generic name for Irish girls away from home. It is an Irish form of Catherine and the 'k' spelling is an anglicisation, since there was no 'k' in the Irish alphabet. The meaning of the name goes back to Greek *katharos*, 'pure'.

Kean, Cian *('keen' or 'kee+an')*

Kean has been adopted in parts of the Americas as a girl's name. It comes from the Irish *cian* and means 'ancient', and implies 'seniority, the wisdom of age'.

Keela *('kee+la')*, Keeley, Keeli, Keely, Kyla *('kie+la')*

The Gaelic word *cadhla* is found mainly in poetry and means 'so beautiful that only poets can describe her'.

Keelin, Caoilfhin(n) *('kale+in')*, Kalin, Kaylinn

These names comes from two Gaelic adjectives, *caol*, 'slender', and *finn*, 'white, fair, pure'.

Kelly

Kelly is a surname associated with Ireland, although it also occurs in the Isle of Man. It may come from *ceallach* and may mean 'hermit' or *ceallúir*, 'churchyard', suggesting perhaps 'steady church-goer'. The meanings of 'red-haired' and 'strife' have also been suggested.

Keri, Kerri, Kerry

Many children of Irish descent have been given this name, especially if a parent or grandparent came from County Kerry. The county name probably means 'country of the Ciarraidhe' or 'country of the children of Ciar'; *ciar* meant 'dark' and probably implied 'dark hair and brown eyes'.

Keri, Kerye

This is the name of a Cornish saint. It is probably related to Welsh Ceri and means 'love'.

Kiera *('key+ra')*, Kira, Kyra

This spelling of the Irish name Ciara is sometimes used as a female form of Ciarán and means 'little dark one'.

Kirstie, Kirsty

Kirstie is a Scottish form of Christina and means 'Christian, follower of Christ'.

Koulm, Koulmia
('cool+em' and 'cool+me+a')

These are Breton names. The first is a female form of *columba*, 'dove', and the second means 'little dove'.

Kylie *('kile+ee')*

Kylie is said to be an Australian Aboriginal word, meaning 'boomerang', and it may have this meaning for most Australian parents. It has, however, also been used as a pet form of Kyle, which may come from the Gaelic words *cill*, 'church', or *coill*, 'wood'.

Lana

Lana is probably a shortened form of Alana, from Irish *a leanbh* and meaning 'darling'.

Lena, Lenaig

The name Helen was adopted by the Bretons in the forms of Lena, Lenaig and Elena. All of the variants come from Greek *helios*, 'sun', and suggest 'sunbeam, ray of light'.

Lesley

Lesley is of Scottish origin and comes from the lands of Lesslyn, a placename that probably means 'grey fort' or 'protector of the grey fort'. The ending '-ley' is used for a girl and '-lie' is preferred for a boy.

Llian *('hlee+an')*

Flax and linen have been important for many years. The Welsh *llian* means 'flax', and 'flaxen' and was often used to describe 'golden' hair.

Madhbh, Maebh, Maeve, Mave, Meadhbh, Medb(h), Meibh *('mayv')*

Madhbh, whose name is usually anglicised to Maeve, was the great warrior queen of Connacht. Her name may be related to *mab*, 'child', or to *meisce* and mean 'the cause of great joy' or 'the cause of great intoxication'. Madhbh's exploits are recorded in the *Táin Bó Cuailgne*, 'The Cattle Raid of Cooley', in which she goes to war with Ulster in order to gain the great brown bull owned by Daire.

Máire, Mair, Mairi, Maisre, Mara, Mari, Maria, Mariam, Marie, Mary, Marya, Maura, May, Melle, Miriam, Moira

It seems likely that Christ's mother

was called Mariam (a variant of Miriam) and that translators from Latin thought of it as the accusative form of 'Maria', a name that she did not have. The name that was used in Ireland for Our Lady was Muire, but this was rarely used as a child's name until the end of the fifteenth century. The Celts did, however, adopt other forms of Mariam and so today we find all the above as well as such diminutives as Maisie, Mamie, Maureen, Molly and Moyenna.

Mairéad *('ma+raid')*, Mairead, Maighread, Mairighead, Muiréad

These are Irish forms of Margaret, which comes from Greek *margaron*, 'pearl'. It was probably borrowed into Gaelic in Norman times from the French form Marguerite. The diminutives Meg and Peg, as well as Meigín and Peigín, are also used.

Maiwen *('my+win')*

This Welsh name may be a blend of *Mair + gwen,* 'beautiful Mary' or *Mai + gwen,* 'beautiful May'.

Maolíosa *('mwel+eesa')*, Melissa

This name has two possible sources. The first is from *maol + Íosa,* 'devotee of Jesus', a name that could be either male or female. The second could be from Celtic words for honey: Welsh has *mel* and Gaelic has *mil.*

Maureen, Maurene, Maurine, Móirín

Maureen comes from Gaelic *Móirín*, meaning 'little Mary'. It is thus a diminutive, but has for centuries been regarded as a name in its own right.

Megan, Meghan *('meg+an')*, Meg

Megan is a Welsh diminutive form

of Margaret, from Greek *margaron*, 'pearl', and thus means 'little pearl'. The form may have been borrowed from, or given rise to such abbreviated forms of Margaret as Meg, Maggie and Mags.

Melanie

Melanie comes from a Greek adjective *melas*, meaning 'black, dark'. It was the name of two fifth-century saints. The name was rarely used outside Cornwall until this century and it was popular there because it overlapped with the Celtic prefix *mal* or *mel*, meaning 'devotee of a saint'.

Melle *('mel+lih' or 'mel')*

This is a Breton form of Mary. The substitution of 'l' for 'r' is found in many languages, including English, where we find both Mary and Molly.

Meredith, Meredyth, Meredydd, Merideth *('mer+id+ith')*

The Welsh surname, Meredith, meaning 'great lord', comes from the given name Maredudd. The name is occasionally shortened to Merry.

Meryl, Muirgheal, Murel, Muriel

These names may come from the Irish *muirgheal*, 'clear as the sea', or from Welsh *muriel*, 'bright as the sea'. However, the forms and the meanings are so close that we may simply have two forms of the one Celtic name. Meryl has possibly been influenced by the French word *merle*, 'blackbird'.

Mona, Monenna

The name Mona is probably more widely used in Ireland than elsewhere. It may come from Gaelic *muadhnaid* or *muadnait* and mean 'noble'; it may have been influenced by the Norman name Monique, 'giver of advice', and it is occasionally used as an abbreviated form of Monica; it may have come from a reduced form of Madonna, 'lady', as in the Mona Lisa; it may even have come from Arabic Mona or Maimona; and finally, it may be from a personification of the moon as Mona.

Morag *('more+ag')*

Morag is a Scottish form of *mór* meaning 'great' plus the ending *ag/óg*, meaning 'young' and so implying 'great young one'. It was virtually unheard of outside Scotland until this century.

Morgan, Morgana, Morganez, Morgane, Morganna, Morrigan

Morgan probably comes from Welsh and may mean 'great queen' or 'bright sea'. The original Morgan or Morrigan was a goddess of war, but one of the best-known Morgans was Morgan le Fay, the daughter of the king of Cornwall, an enemy of King Arthur.

Moya, Moyenna

Moya is a variant of Máire but it has been used so widely that it has gained the status of a name in its own right. Moyenna is like a blend of Moya and either Anna, meaning 'graceful', or Enya, meaning 'flame'.

Muirne *('moor+nyih')*, Murine *('moor+een')*, Myrna

Murine, which may be from *muirne*, 'beloved', or *máthair* + Fionn, meaning 'mother of Fionn', was the sister-in-law of Lugh and the mother of Fionn MacCool. She gave birth to Fionn after the death of her husband and left the child in the care of a female druid and a female warrior.

Nan, Nana, Nanna

Nanna is one of the words like 'Mama' that occurs in virtually every culture. It is sometimes used in Ireland as a form of Áine and can also be related to *naonúr*, 'nine'. However, Nan(n)a was also an ancient goddess of flowers and this fact may have influenced the popularity of Nan(n)a.

Neasa, Nessa

Nessa was the wife of Cathbad and the mother of Conchubhar. Her name was originally Assa, meaning 'gentle', but, to defend her people, she took up arms against Cathbad and was so successful that her name was changed to Ní Assa, 'not gentle'.

Nerys *('ner+iss')*

Nerys is the female form of Welsh *ner*, 'lord', and thus means 'lady'.

Nesta

Nesta may be a Latinised form of Nest, the Welsh pet form of Agnes, which comes from Greek *hagnos*, meaning 'pure, holy'. The 'h' from *hagnos* was lost when the name was equated with Latin *agnus*, meaning 'lamb'.

Niamh *('nee+iv' or 'neev')*

Niamh of the Golden Hair was the daughter of Manannan, the god of the sea. She was extraordinarily beautiful. She fell in love with Fionn's son, Oisín, and took him to live with her in Tír na nÓg. Her name, Niamh, means 'radiance, brightness' and it is close in form to *naomh*, the Irish word for 'saint'.

Nola, Noleen, Nolwenn

Nola and Noleen are usually considered to be abbreviated forms of Fin(n)ola, a variant of Fionnuala. They may come from a Celtic name Nola, 'famous', and are similar to the Breton saint's name, Nolwenn.

Nora, Norah, Noreen

Nora is a shortened form of Latin Honora, 'honour'. The form 'Norah' was influenced by such Biblical names as Sarah. Noreen is a blend of Nora and the Irish diminutive marker -*ín* and so means 'little honourable one'.

Oanez *('wan+ez')*

Oanez is a Breton form of Agnes, a name that came originally from Greek *hagnos*, 'pure, holy', and was reinforced by Latin *agnus*, 'lamb'.

Odhrán, Oran *('o+ran')*, Orin, Orna *('or+na')*

These names are variants of *odhra*, meaning 'dark haired'. There are several saints called Orna and one may have set up a Christian settlement in Iona before Columbanus.

Olwen, Olwyn, Olwynne *('ol+win')*

Olwen is a Welsh name from *ol* + *gwen*, 'footprint + white'. According to one legend, Olwen was the daughter of a giant called Yspaddadyn and was so beautiful that white clover grew wherever she put her foot.

Orla, Órla, Órfhlaith, Orlaith *('or+la')*

Orla means 'golden lady' and the meaning helps to explain the popularity of the name. Orla could also come from the Irish *ór*, 'golden' + *snaith*, 'thread'.

Pádraigín, Paidrigín *('paw+drig+een')*, Paddy, Paití, Patricia, Pat, Patsy

These names are female versions of Padraig and Patrick, both forms of *patricius*, 'of noble birth', which is Latin, not Celtic. The pet names Paddy, Paití, Pat and Patsy are perhaps even more common in Ireland than Patricia.

Peggy, Peig, Peigín
('peg', 'peg+een')

These names are usually described as forms of Margaret, coming from Greek *margaros*, meaning 'pearl'. Peggy (and Maggie) are used in Ireland, the Isle of Man and Scotland.

Q

The early Celtic alphabets did not use 'q' and so it is unusual in Celtic names. It does, however, occur as an alternative spelling for the initial cluster 'kw' as in 'Quinn'.

Quinnie, Queenie

Quinnie has been used as a female form of Quinn, which probably comes from the name Conn, meaning 'intelligence'. It can also be a variant of Kinnie, a Breton name associated with the defeat of darkness over light. Her feast day is celebrated, like St Brigid's, on 1 February. Occasionally, Queenie is used.

R

Rae *('ray')*

Rae is most popular in Australia where it has been related to the Gaelic phrase *rae beag mná*, 'little woman' or to *rae*, 'moon'. Rae could also be a reduced form of Raymond, with the spelling modified to suggest a girl.

Rhiannon, Riwanon
('hree+an+on', 'ree+wan+on')

Rhiannon is Welsh and means 'nymph' or 'moon goddess'. She is sometimes also called Rigantona, 'great queen'. In Welsh literature, Rhiannon was the daughter of the king of the Underworld. She was exceptionally beautiful as well as being a fine horsewoman.

Rhona, Rona *('ro+na')*

No-one is certain when this name began to be used as a girl's name although it was certainly popular in Scotland during the nineteenth century. The spelling with 'h' has been influenced by 'Rhoda', which comes from Greek 'rose' or 'woman from Rhodes'. It is also possible that Rona is from Gaelic *rón*, meaning 'seal'.

Rhonda *('ron + da')*

Rhonda looks Welsh and could be from *rhodd*, 'gift'. It may also have been influenced by the name of the Rhondda Valley, one of the coal-mining regions in Wales.

Ríona *('ree+in+a')*, Ríonach

This name comes from the Irish *ríon*, 'queen' and means 'like a queen'.

Róisín *('rosh+een')*

Róisín means 'little rose' and, as *roisín*, 'balm, comforter'. It has been used as a name for Ireland for five centuries and James Clarence Mangan translated a sixteenth-century poem, 'Róisín Dubh', as 'Dark Rosaleen'.

Rori, Ruairí
('ro+ree' and 'roo+ir+ee')

Rori comes from Irish *ruadhraí*, meaning 'red-headed ruler'. It is used as a feminine form of Rory.

Rowena *('ro+ween+na')*

Many people who read Sir Walter Scott's novel *Ivanhoe* were captivated by the character and beauty of Lady Rowena. Scott may have made up the name, possibly as an anology with 'Rowan', from Gaelic *ruadhán*, meaning 'little red one', or it may be a Germanic name meaning 'fame and joy'.

Rozenn ('ro+zen')

Rozenn is a Breton name meaning 'rose'. The rose is not only a beautiful flower, it has, for centuries, been associated with mysticism

S

Sadhbh, Sive ('sigh've')

Sadhbh's name means 'goodness, sweetness'. It is related to modern Irish *sáimhe*, 'peacefulness, tranquillity'. She was transformed into a deer because she refused to marry Fionn MacCool, a man she did not love.

Saoirse ('seer+shih' or 'sare+shih')

Saoirse is a relatively new name in the Celtic tradition, used since the 1920s, and is Irish for 'freedom'.

Saraid ('sor+id')

Saraid is related to the Irish *sár* and implies 'best, surpassing all'. The earliest record we have of the name is as the daughter of Conn of the Hundred Battles.

Selma

Selma is probably from a Celtic word meaning 'fair, beautiful'. It is likely that it has been influenced by Anselm, a name that means 'God's helmet' and also, possibly, by Hebrew *shalom*, 'peace'.

Seonaid ('shone+aid') ('o+ran'), Sinéad ('shin+aid'), Shaynee

These names are Gaelic forms of Jeannette or Janet, the first from Scotland and the second from Ireland. The Normans introduced the name as a feminine form of Jean, meaning 'John', a name of Hebrew origin implying 'God is gracious'.

Seve, Seva ('sev', 'se+va')

These are Breton names that are probably related to Sadhbh and suggest 'peace, tranquillity'.

45

Shanna, Shannagh, Shannan, Shannen, Shannon

These names are all probably derived from the River Shannon, which is related to *sean*, 'old', and means 'the old one'.

Sheena, Síne *('shee+nih')*

Sheena is an anglicised spelling of Síne, a Scots Gaelic form of 'Jeanne' or 'Jane'. All of these names are feminine forms of John, which means 'God is gracious'.

Sheila, Sheela, Sheelagh, Síle

It is probable that Sheila is an Irish form of Cecilia, the patron saint of music, and so implies 'pure and musical', but it may have been influenced by the Hebrew name Shelah, meaning 'longed-for'.

Shibley, Sibéal
('shib+lee', 'shib+ale')

Shibley and Sibéal are forms of Isabel, which is a Spanish form of the Hebrew name Elisheba, meaning 'God is my oath'. Forms of Elizabeth have been popular throughout the Celtic world.

Sian *('shan')*

Sian is the Welsh equivalent of Gaelic Síne and they are both forms of 'Jeanne' or 'Jane', names that were popularised by the Normans and became even more widely used in the Celtic areas after the death of Jeanne d'Arc or Joan of Arc.

Siobhán *('shiv+aun')*, Shevaun, Chevonne, Siubhan, Siún *('shoo+win')*

Siobhán is one of the best-known Gaelic names for girls. The name has been anglicised as Shevaun and Shivaun, and frenchified as

Chevonne. All of these names are versions of Susan, meaning 'lily', or Joan, meaning 'God is gracious'.

Sorcha *('sor+ha')*

Sorcha is a traditional Gaelic name, *sorcha* meaning 'brightness, light'. It is often regarded as the Irish equivalent of Sarah, a name that means 'princess', although there is no actual link between the names.

T

Tamsin, Tamasin, Tamzin

Tamsin is a modified form of Thomasina, and thus means 'female twin' and was once popular throughout the British Isles, but mostly in Cornwall.

Tara

Tara was originally the name of a royal prehistoric fort in Co. Meath dating back 4,000 years. Its meaning is not known but it possibly implies 'crag, hill' and is therefore related to modern Irish *tor* which means 'bulging hill', found in such Celtic placenames as Torquay in Devon and Torpoint in Cornwall.

Tegan *('teg+an')*

Tegan is a Welsh name, related to *tegwch*, 'beauty', and meaning 'beautiful'.

Trac(e)y, Trea, Treasa
('tray+see', 'tray+a', 'trass+a')

These names are usually thought of as Irish forms of Teresa, the name of several saints, including St Teresa of Avila. However, they may be from an Irish noun *treise* that meant 'strength'. Teresa itself has many other abreviations including Teezy, Teri, Terry and Tré.

Trina, Triona *('tree+(i)na')*

Trina and Triona are abbreviations of Catrina and Caitríona and so are indirectly related to Hecate, a Greek goddess of enchantment and to the Greek word *katharos*, meaning 'pure'.

U

Una, Úna, Oona, Oonagh *('oo+na')*

Una is often translated as Unity because of the meaning of Latin *una*, 'one', but it appears to be an indigenous Gaelic name possibly associated with 'banshee'.

V, X, Y, Z

Early Celtic alphabets did not make use of these letters and so we do not find many examples of traditional names beginning with them.

W

Wendy

Wendy is sometimes regarded as an abbreviation of Gwendoline, but it seems that the Scottish playwright, JM Barrie, coined it for one of the characters in *Peter Pan* because he had heard a child call another 'my fwendy' (my friend)!

Winifred, Wynne

Winifred is a Germanic name meaning 'gracious friend' but it is often equated with the name of a seventh-century Welsh saint, Gwenfrewi, meaning 'fair + reconciliation' and with Wynne, from Welsh *gwen*, meaning 'fair', or *gwyn*, meaning 'blessed'.

Y

Yanna

Yanna is a female form of Yann and has occurred in Brittany and Cornwall. It means 'God is gracious'.

Boys'
Names

A

Adair, A'dair

This name comes from the same root as Gaelic *doire*, meaning 'oak grove', a place sacred to the Celts.

Aed(h), Aodh *('ay')*

It seems likely that Aed(h) was a god of fire. The Gaelic word *aodh* means 'fire, flame'. It was also the name of a sixth-century Irish saint and an eighth-century high king.

Ael *('ell', 'ale')*

The Breton name for the saint of 5 May is Ael; there is also a feminine form Aela. Little is known about the original Ael but the name may be connected with rocks or a rampart – the Celts often built forts on high hills.

Aengus, Angus, Aonghus *('eng+iss', 'ang+gus')*

The first and third spellings are found mostly in Ireland, and Angus is the preferred Scottish form. Aengus, sometimes called Aengus Óg, was the god of love and poetry. The name probably means 'outstanding, exceptional'.

Aidan, Aod(h)án *('aid+in', 'aid+on')*, Edan

It seems that these are diminutive forms of Aedh and Aodh, and come from *aodh*, 'fire', but they have became names in their own right in honour of the seventh-century Irish saint who carried Christianity to Northumbria. Aidan is associated with strength of mind and courage of heart.

Alan, Alain, Allan, Allen, Alun

It seems likely that this is a Breton name, related to *alp*, meaning 'rock', although it is possible that it has been reinforced by a Gaelic meaning of 'cheerful and harmonious'. Alan gave rise to the surnames Allan and Allen, both of which were subsequently used as first names. The form with 'u' is almost exclusively Welsh.

Alaisdair, Alaister, Alasdair, Alastair, Aleister, Alisder, Alister, Alusdur

There are numerous spellings of this Scots Gaelic form of Alexander, which probably comes from Greek *alexein* + *aner*, 'to defend' + 'man', implying 'warrior'.

Aled, Aleid *('a+lid' with the main stress on 'a')*

Aled has become popular in Wales. It may mean 'noble brow' but carries with it overtones of contemporary Welsh *alaeth*, 'sorrow'.

Andrew, Andrev, Aindrias

These are forms of Greek Andreas, meaning 'brave, manly, virile'. Andrew was the first apostle called by Jesus and he is the patron saint of Scotland. The English form Andrew is widely used, as are Andie and Andy; Andrev is preferred in Brittany, and Aindrias is found in Gaelic-speaking areas.

Ardal, Ardghal
('awe+r+gal')

This name may have a long Celtic heritage. It is possible that it comes from a combination of the Irish words *árd* + *geal* implying 'high courage'. It is also possible that it is a form of Art or Arthur: the 'l' instead of 'r' in Arthur was widely found in Brittany and Wales.

Arlen

Arlen was an early Cornish saint, probably related to Elwin, a name that means 'kind and handsome'.

Art

An early Irish use of Art is found in the name of Cormac MacAirt, a legendary high king of Ireland. The name Art may come originally from Greek *arktourous*, 'keeper of bears', because the bear was sacred to all the Celts. It may also derive from an old Gaelic word *art*, 'stone'. It is also possible that it is the male equivalent of Artio, a Celtic bear goddess. Bears were found all over Europe when the Celts were the dominant tribe.

Arthur, Artúr *('art+oor')*, Arzhul *('are+zool')*

In the anglicised form Arthur, this name is known because of the stories about King Arthur and the Knights of the Round Table. Like Art, the name may owe its origin to Greek *arktourous*, 'keeper of bears'. In the Celtic languages, however, it probably means 'bear' or 'strong as a bear'. Another possible origin is *art*, 'bear', + *úr*, 'fresh, pure'.

Auryn *('aw+rin')*

The Welsh, like the other Celts, probably took their word for 'gold' from Latin. *Aur* means 'gold' and Auryn implies 'golden one'.

B

Barra, Barris, Barry, Baz, Bazza, Bearach

These Gaelic names all seem to be related and probably come from *bearach*, meaning 'spear' and implying 'warrior'. Barry is used both as a given name and a surname, and the 'z' forms are found mostly in Australia and in the southeast of England. Barry is the English form of Fionnbharr; Finbar means 'fairheaded Barry'. The Welsh name Barris means 'Barry's son'.

Bernard, Bernez

Bernard was popularised by the Normans and may have appealed to the Celts because it meant 'brave, hardy bear'. The bear was admired by the Celts for its strength and courage. The forms Bernie, Barnie and Barney are used as diminutives, as is Barn in Australia. Bernez occurs in Brittany.

Bevan, Bevin *('bev+an')*

This Welsh name is an anglicised form of *ap* + Evan, 'son of God's gracious gift'.

Blair

The name Blair occurs mainly in Scotland as both a first name and a surname. It seems to come from *blár*, meaning 'plain' and suggesting 'one from the plains'.

Blaise, Bleiz

There are at least two Blaises in Celtic tradition. The former was a magician who trained Merlin and who had the gift of second sight; this name may be related to Irish *blas*, 'taste, flavour', which may partly account for the tradition

that Blaise can heal sore throats. The other is a Saint Blaise o Blasins, a martyred doctor, renowned for his kindness to animals. The form Bleiz is found in Brittany and there is a town called St Blazey in Cornwall.

Bradie, Brady

These names derive from the Irish surname, which may come from *bradán*, 'salmon', or they may have been from English 'broad + ey', meaning 'island'.

Bran

Bran is an old Celtic word *bran(n)*, meaning 'raven', a bird that was sacred to all the Celts and may have been a harbinger of death. The name has been held by a Welsh giant-like god who possessed a liquid that could restore life (whiskey = the water of life); by an Irish navigator who found an island inhabited only by women; and by Fionn MacCool's wolfhound. Names like Brannagan and Brannigan are diminutives of Bran.

Brannagh *('branna')*

Among the Anglo-Norman invaders of Ireland in the twelfth century were some Welsh men, whom the Irish called Breathnach or 'Welshman'. The name became a surname, Brannagh, and then a first name. Its move towards a given name was helped by the fact that *bran*, 'raven', was a sacred bird among the Celts and carried the secondary meaning of 'chieftain'.

Brannoc, Brannock Brynach

It seems that Brannoc's name is related to *bran + ieuanc*, meaning 'young raven'. Brannoc came from the royal house of Calabria in Italy but worked as a priest in sixth-century Cornwall. He is known as Brannoc in Cornwall, and as Brynach in Wales. There is also an early Breton saint, Branwalader, who may be the same person.

Brendan, Brandan, Brandon, Breandán

Versions of this name are found in all of the Celtic regions, and Brittany celebrates his feast day on 16 May. There are at least 16 saints who bear this name, but many of the legends are about Brendan the Navigator. He seems to have been born in Kerry, although his name may come from a Welsh word *brenin*, meaning 'king'. Tradition has it that he set sail in a small boat with a group of monks in the early sixth century and was the first European to visit America.

Brett, Bret

Brett may be a form of Breiz, 'Brittany', suggesting 'native of Brittany', but it might also come from *ap* + Rhett, 'son of the ardent one'.

Briac ('bree+ack'), Briag, Briagenn

These are Breton forms of Brian, meaning 'noble, strong'.

Brian, Briant, Brion, Bryan

This name has become popular all over the world and seems to come from *brígh*, meaning 'noble, strong, virtuous'.

Brice, Bryce

These are forms of Welsh *ap + rhys*, 'son of the ardent one'. It is also possible that the name is from an older Celtic word meaning 'alert'.

Brodie, Brody

Brodie comes from Scots Gaelic *brothaigh*, 'rampart'. It is possible that this name goes back to Pictish.

Bruce

The meaning of this name is probably 'Brix, France' or 'Bruges, Belgium'. Bruce became linked to Scotland because of Robert the Bruce, who became King of Scotland in 1306 and defeated the English at Bannockburn in 1314.

Bryn

The Welsh name Bryn, meaning 'hill', may have contributed to the popularity of Brian. Bryn is popular in Wales and Cornwall.

C

Caddock, Cado, Cadoc, Cadog, Kadec, Kadeg

Caddock probably comes from *cathach*, meaning 'brave in battle'. The life of St Cadoc, or Cadog, was written in Wales in the twelfth century: he was a prince, the son of Gwynllyh and Gwladys, became abbot of Llancarfan, and travelled widely in Cornwall, Ireland, Scotland and Brittany. He was extremely popular in Wales and Cornwall in the Middle Ages, and seems also to have had followers in Brittany, where the variants Cado, Cadoc, Kadec and Kadeg are still used and where the meaning is sometimes related to French *cadeau*, 'present, gift'.

Cael ('kale' in Ireland, 'kile' in Wales)

In Gaelic, the adjective *caol* means 'slender'; in Welsh *cael* means 'have'.

Cahal, Cathal ('ka+hal')

This traditional Gaelic name comes from *cathal* and means 'powerful in battle'. It has various spellings including, occasionally, Kathal. Although it is not related to Charles or Carolus, it is often translated into English as 'Charles'.

Cahir, Cathaoir ('ka+here')

This name is from *cathair*, 'guard'. It is related to Cathal and was the name of a High King of Ireland.

Cai, Kai, Kaie, Kay, Kaye, Ke, Quay ('kay')

This is the name of King Arthur's foster brother. The name may be related to the Welsh word, *cad*, for 'battle', or it may be a form of the Latin name Gaius. It is also found in Brittany, where it occurs in the forms Ke, Kaie and Quay.

Callum, Calum

Callum, with either a single or double 'l', is a Scottish form of Colm and comes from Latin *columba*, meaning 'dove'.

Cameron, Camryn

The Camerons are a Scottish Highland clan renowned for courage and resourcefulness. The name, used both as a surname and a given name, seems to come from the nickname meaning 'crooked nose', from *cam*, 'crooked', and *srón*, 'nose'.

Canice, Coinneach

('can+iss' and 'kin+noch')

Canice seems to be from Gaelic *coinneach*, 'attractive person'. Coinneach was a sixth-century Irish missionary priest and founder of Cill Choinnigh (Kilkenny), whose cathedral is St Canice's. Coinneach was better known in Britain by his Latin name Canicus, or as Kenneth in Scotland.

Carey, Cary *('care+ee')*

The name of the river Cary in Somerset is of Celtic origin, possibly *car*, meaning 'well loved', or perhaps more likely 'stony' or 'castle dweller'. A second source of this name is the Irish surname Carey or Cary. This name may come from the Gaelic word *ciar*, meaning 'dark'. The third source may be the Welsh word *caer*, for 'fort, castle', found in such place-names as Caernarvon.

Carrick, Carrig, Craig

These names come from the Gaelic word *carraig* for 'rock'. Craig is the most widely used version.

Carroll, Cearúil, Cearbhall, Carl, Karl

These are versions of an ancient name *cearbhall*, probably meaning 'fierce warrior'.

Casey

From the Irish surname Casey, and probably comes from *cathasach* and means 'war vigilant'.

Cass(idy)

The Irish surname Cassidy is of uncertain meaning, although it may be from *cas*, 'curly haired'. There is a folk tradition that a Cassidy was always the doctor for the O'Neill clan.

Cecil

Cecil comes ultimately from an

old Welsh name *seissylt*, meaning 'sixth', given to a sixth child. Later, it became the surname of a family that rose to power under Elizabeth I. Later still, it became popular as a first name.

Cedric

The name Cedric seems to have been used first by Sir Walter Scott in his novel *Ivanhoe*. It may be of Celtic origin, related to *céadrith*, and mean 'first choice', or it may simply have been made up.

Cerwyn

This Welsh name from *car* + *gwyn* means 'fair love'.

Cian, Cane, Kane, Kean, Keane

These names possibly come from different sources but have reinforced each other. Cian probably comes from Gaelic *cian*, meaning 'ancient', and is used for both boys

and girls, especially in the form of Kean. The Gaelic name Cathán, meaning 'warrior', gave rise to the surnames Kane and O'Kane which, in their turn, encouraged Cane and Kane as given names.

Ciarán ('kee+er+awn'), Kieran, Kieron, Keiran, Ceran, Queran

These names are the most frequently used variants of Gaelic Ciarán, meaning 'little dark one'. The name has been popular for over 1,500 years and at least 26 saints have borne it. One of the best known was the abbot of Clonmacnoise, and his feast day is celebrated in Brittany on 5 March.

Cillian, Killian

This name may come from *cill,* 'church', and mean 'associated with the church', or *ciall,* 'good sense'. It is popular in Ireland but also in both France and Germany, where two Irish Cillians worked as missionaries. The forms Kilian and Kilien are preferred in Brittany.

Colin, Coll, Collen, Cul(l)an, Cullen, Coilín

There are a number of explanations for these names. Coll(a), from *coll*, meaning 'high, chieftain', has been used in Scotland and Ireland and was reinforced by the use of Col as a medieval diminutive of the Greek form of Nicholas, meaning 'people's victory'. The Gaelic words *caileán* and *coileán*, meaning 'cub, young one', may well have resulted in the popularity of Colin and Cullen as first names.

Colm, Colum, Colmcille, Columb, Columba, Coulm, Colman, Kolman

All these are variants of Latin *columba*, meaning 'dove'; there are over 30 saints whose name has been a form of this. The dove symbolised peace, purity and the Holy Spirit, and was used in all areas of the Celtic world. Colman is a form of the name Columbanus. As well as several hundred Irish saints called Colman, the name has been given to poets and priests, musicians and missionaries. St Columba was also called *colm + cille*, Colmcille, or 'dove of the church'. He was born in Northern Ireland about 521 and became a monk under St Finnian.

Conaire, Conchobar, Conchubhar, Conchúr, Conchobarre *('con+or', or 'con+oo+er')*, Conor

These names are all variants of Con(n)or and may come from *conairt*, 'pack of hounds', and imply 'lover of hounds' or *conáire*, meaning 'hound-nobleman'. There are many Irish Conors – some saints, many sinners and at least two kings: Conaire, king of Tara, and Conchubhar MacNessa, king of Ulster.

Conall, Connall, Connell

This name comes from Irish *con*, a prefix relating to 'hound' and meaning 'strong as an (Irish) hound'.

Conan, Konan

This Gaelic name is probably a diminutive form of *con(n)* and, in the form *cónán*, means 'little wolf-hound'. Konan is the preferred form in Brittany.

Conn

This was originally a name in its own right, in that the Irish word *conn* could mean 'noble one', but it is often thought to be a reduced form of Connor or Conall or Constantine.

Corey, Cory

Corey, like many Irish surnames, was originally a first name, probably derived from the Germanic name *god* + *frid(d)*, Godfrey, meaning 'God's peace'. Its use may have been encouraged in Ireland by the Gaelic *cuairteoir*, 'visitor'.

Cormac, Cormack, Cormick

Cormac comes from *cor* + *mac* and means 'son of the raven'. The name is especially popular in Ireland and Scotland. There are several early references to Cormacs: one was the high king of Ireland, Cormac Mac Airt, and another was the warrior son of Conchubhar MacNessa.

Cronán, Cronin

Cronán seems to come from *crón* and to mean 'sallow, dark-complexioned'. The seventh-century saint Cronán dedicated his life to the poor and the homeless.

Cullan, Cullen, Cullin

It is likely that this name is a diminutive of *coll*, 'chieftain'.

D

Dacey

The name comes from Gaelic *deas* and means 'southern'.

Dai, Dáibhí, Dafydd, Davet, David, Davie, Davy, Devi, Dewi, Divi, Tafydd

David was the name of the king of the Israelites, as told in the Book of Samuel. It means 'beloved, darling' and has been popular worldwide. The patron saint of Wales is David and Scotland had two kings with the name. Dáibhí, Davet, David, Davie and Davy are used in Ireland; Devi, Divi and Dewi occur in Brittany; Dafydd, David, Davie, Davy, Dewi and Tafydd are used in Wales; and Scotland and the Isle of

Man tend to use David, Davie and Davy. The Welsh pronunciation of Dafydd was often heard as Tafydd.

Dáire *('daw+ir+ih')*, Darry, Dary

Dáire was a Gaelic god, whose name, *dáire*, means 'fruitful'.

Dáithí *('dah+hee', 'daw+hee')*, Dahey, Dahy, Dathy

Dáithí is sometimes interpreted as a form of Dáibhí, but Gaelic *daithe* mean 'swiftness, nimbleness'. It was the name of a fifth-century Irish king whose warlike adventures are similar to those of King Arthur.

Dara *('dar+ra')*, Darach, Daragh, Darrach, Darragh

These variants all come from a Gaelic word *dara*, meaning 'like oak'. The '*-ach*' forms are popular in Scotland and the others are preferred in Ireland.

Daren, Darin, Darran, Darren

This name is most likely a diminutive of *dara* and means 'little oak'.

Deaglán, Declán

('deg+lawn', 'deck+lawn'), **Declan** *('deck + lan')*

Deaglán or Declan seems to have been one of the first Irish Christians and may have preached in Ireland before the arrival of St Patrick. It is not certain what the name means although it may be related to *deagh*, 'good', + *lán*, 'full', suggesting 'full of goodness'.

Derry

Derry is used as an abbreviation of Andrew, Derek, Dermot and, less often, Desmond, but it has a meaning in its own right and, as *daraigh*, can suggest 'like an oak'.

Desmond, Deasmhumhain *('dass+oon')*, Deasún

Desmond was originally an Irish regional classification meaning 'one from south Munster, or Deas Mumhan'. The anglicised ending is due to influence from such names as Esmond and Richmond. Desmond has several popular diminutives, including Des, Dessie, Desy, Dez and Dezzy.

Diarmad, Diarmaid, Diarmait, Diarmid, Diarmuid, Dermot, Dermott

This name occurs in a wide number of forms. The Diar- forms are found in Scotland, Ireland and, to a lesser extent, the Isle of Man, and the Der- forms are popular worldwide as both first names and, with Mac, as surnames. The name probably comes from *di + airmait*, meaning 'without envy', and it has been held by warriors, kings and saints.

Dillon

Dillon may be related to *dealán*, 'streak of light', or it may mean 'faithful, loyal'. It is widely used as a surname in Ireland and is occasionally equated with Welsh Dylan.

Domhnal(l), Donal, Donald

At one time Donald was second only to Ian as the most popular male name in Scotland. The earlier form of the Gaelic name, Domhnal(l), helps us to see its meaning of 'ruler of the world' in that *domhan* is 'world'.

Donncha *('done+ah+ha')*, Donnchadh, Don(n)ach, Don(n)agh, Don(n)ough

These names are variants of a Gaelic noun *donnchadh*, meaning

'brown-haired warrior'. They are found in versions of the surname Donaghy.

Donovan

Like many ancient Irish first names, Donovan was preserved by becoming a surname. It is a combination of *donn*, meaning 'brown' or 'princely', and *dubh*, meaning 'black', plus a diminutive marker, suggesting that it may have been a nickname originally, meaning either 'little dark one' or 'little dark prince'.

Dougal, Dubhgal(l), Dugald

The Irish distinguished between the Viking invaders from Norway, the *fionn* + *gall*, meaning 'fair stranger', and the Danes, the *dubh* + *gall*, meaning 'dark stranger', leading to Dougal, which became a popular first name, especially in Scotland. It seems likely that the surname

Doyle is a form of Dubhgall and it, too, has been used as a given name.

Douglas

The name Douglas comes from the Gaelic elements *dubh* + *glas,* meaning 'black + water', a name that was given to several rivers and to the capital of the Isle of Man. It is used also as a surname in Scotland, where the Douglas clan has been powerful since the twelfth century.

Duncan

Duncan is a form of *donn* + *cha(dh),* meaning 'princely battle' or, more likely, 'brown-haired warrior'. It is most popular in Scotland, where it was the name of the king murdered by Macbeth. It was also held by both an Irish and a Scottish saint.

Dylan

Dylan probably comes from a poetic Welsh noun meaning 'sea'.

He was the son of Arianrhod, who taught poets. More recently, the name has been held by the Welsh poet, Dylan Thomas.

E

Eamon, Éamon, Eamonn, Éamonn
('aim+an')

Eamon(n) is the Irish equivalent of Old English *ead* + *mund*, Edmond or Edmund, and the name means 'prosperity and protection'.

Egan, Egin, Eginer, Iagan *('ey+gan', 'ee+gan')*

Originally, Egan was written Aodhgan and was probably a pet form of Aodh or Aidan, and thus meant 'little fire'. The name has given rise to the surnames Hagan and O'Hagan, and Hagan is occasionally used as a first name too. There is a Scottish form Iagan and a Breton equivalent Eginer, which also has Fingar as a pet form.

Éibhear *('aye+ver')*, Eber

Éibhear and his brother were reputed to be Milesians, or early settlers in Ireland. Éibhear is an Irish version of Latin Hibernia, 'winter country'; though scholars now dispute legends of settlement, the name has survived. Yves is occasionally used as a variant of Éibhear.

Ellis, Elisud, Eliaz

Ellis is a Welsh name, thought to be a reduced form of *elisud*, which means 'benevolent'. The Welsh name has been influenced in spelling by the English surname Ellis, which comes from the Biblical Elias or Elijah, meaning 'Jehovah is God'. There is a Breton form Eliaz.

Elwin, Elouan

Elwin occurs as a first name and may be a blend of Welsh *elus* + *gwyn*, meaning 'kind + fair'. Its Breton equivalent is Elouan, and the names are very close in pronunciation.

Emmet

Emmet is an example of a name that is Irish by adoption, thanks to the patriot Robert Emmet. The name Emmet is an English surname and comes from an Old English word *oemette*, 'ant'.

Enda, Éanna

This comes from Gaelic *éan*, meaning 'bird'. The best-known Enda was a warrior and a monk in the sixth century. He trained in Ireland and in Galloway, Scotland, then returned to Ireland.

Eoghan, Eoin *('oh+wen')*, Erwan, Euan, Ewen, Owen

Variants of this name occur in all parts of the Celtic world. We have Eoghan in Ireland and Scotland, Ewen and Owen in Wales, Ewen and Youenn in Brittany, Eoin in Ireland and the Isle of Man, and the variants overlap with forms of John. It is uncertain where the name originated. It seems likely that it may have come from an old Celtic word for 'yew tree' and it may have been influenced by the name Eugene, which comes from Greek *eugenios*, meaning 'noble', and was held by a seventh-century pope.

Ernan, Ernie, Iarnan

This name comes from the Gaelic word *iarann*, 'iron', a metal that was held in high esteem by Celts for its durability. The name is now often linked with Ernest, a Germanic name meaning 'seriousness'.

Evan, Evin, Even

Evan is considered to be Welsh, a form of John, meaning 'God is gracious'. Evan and Even are used also in Brittany where they are linked with John the Baptist. These forms overlap in Ireland and Scotland with forms of Eoghan, which are sometimes Ewan, Euan or Ewen. The Irish Evin does not seem to be related historically, since it means 'swift', but it is usual now to equate the names.

F

Fanch, Fransez, Soaz

These are all Breton forms of Francis, meaning 'Frenchman' or 'from France'.

Faolán *('fway+lawn')*, Felan, Phelan *('feel+an')*

Faolán may come from *faoile-ann*, 'seagull', although it is often claimed to mean 'wolf'.

Fearghal *('fer+gull')*, Fergal, Farrell, Ferrel(l)

There is some debate about the meaning of Fergal but it seems to be from *fearghal* and to mean 'brave, courageous, valorous'. Farrell is an anglicisation of Fergal and occurs widely in Ireland as a surname.

Fearghas, Fearghus, Feargus, Fergus
('far+a+gas' or 'fer+guss')

The meaning of these names is debated but is probably derived from *fearr*, 'best', or *fear*, 'man', or *fearr + gas*, 'best warrior'. The first variant is used mainly in Ireland, the second in Scotland, but Fergus is the preferred form worldwide. According to legend, Fergus was the king of Ulster.

Ferdia, Ferdiad

The meaning of this name is not certain but it may come from *fear + Dia* and mean 'man of God'. What is certain is that he and Cúchulainn were close friends, but were forced to meet in single combat in the Táin Bó Cuailgne, where Cúchulainn won.

Fiachna *('fee+ach+nah')*

Fiachna seems to be a version of *fiach*, 'raven'. He was the son of king Lír and brother of Fionnuala.

Fiachra, Fiacre, Fiakr
('fee+ach+rih')

These variants are found in Ireland and Brittany. Fiachra comes from *fiach*, meaning 'raven', a bird that was sacred to the Celts, and an early Irish hermit called Fiachra went to live in Northern France.

Finan, Fíonán

This Gaelic name seems to be from Latin *vinum*, 'wine', although it may have been influenced by *fionn*, meaning 'white, fair'.

Finbar, Fionnbar(r), Fymber

This name probably comes from *fi(o)nn + bearr*, meaning 'fair-headed'. The name has been popular since the sixth century and

St Finbar of Cork had cult status in Cornwall, under the name of Fymber.

Finn, Fionn

Finn or Fionn means 'fair-haired' and the most famous Fionn to date is Fionn MacCool, the legendary leader of the Fianna. Fionn was not only incredibly strong, but he was also extremely wise.

Finnian, Finian

Finnian is thought to mean 'fair-headed' and it may be a blend of Gaelic *finn* and Welsh or Cornish *gwyn*.

Fintan, Fiontan

Fintan is one of the many Gaelic names coming from *finn* or *fionn* and referring to fair hair. It is the equivalent of 'fair-haired one'. There have been many saints with this name.

Flann, Flannagan

Flann means 'bright red' and its use was popularised by the writer Flann O'Brien. Flannagan is a pet form of the name.

Floyd

Floyd is a variant of Lloyd, from Welsh *llwyd*, meaning 'grey-haired'.

Fraser, Frazier, Frizzell

The Frasers were originally Normans from La Fraselière in France. The 'l' in the name accounts for the fact that the Frasers were called Friseal in Gaelic, a name that can mean 'fresh'.

G

Gael *('gale')*

Gael occurs as a first name in Brittany and probably comes from *gaedheal*, meaning 'Irish'. The variants Gail and Kelig are also found.

Gair ('gare')

Gair is occasionally found in Scotland. It was originally a nickname meaning 'short', coming from Gaelic *gearr*.

Galaher, Gallagher, Gallaher ('gal+a+her')

These names all come from Gaelic *gall*, 'foreign', + *cabhair*, 'help', and mean 'foreign help'.

Galvin

Galvin may come from *geal* + *finn* or *fionn* and mean 'very white, fair' or it may be a form of 'sparrow' from Gaelic *gealbhán*.

Garbhán ('gar+vawn'), Garvin, Gervan, Gervin, Girvin, Gurvan

Garbhán comes from *garbh*, 'rough to the touch' and means 'rugged'; the Gurvan form seems to be confined to Brittany.

Gareth ('ga+rith')

Gareth is often thought to be a Welsh form of Gerald, however it seems to come from Welsh *gwared*, meaning 'gentle'.

Garret(t), Gearóid ('gar+rode'), Gerrit, Giraud

Gerald was introduced into the Celtic areas by the Normans. The name is related to Gerard, which comes from *gar* + *wald*, 'spear' + 'rule' and means 'noble warrior' or 'spear carrier'. Gareth is popular in Wales and Cornwall and is often regarded as being related to Garret or Garrett, which are frequently used in Ireland. All of them can be abbreviated to Gar, Gary or Garry. The forms Gerrit and Giraud have been recorded in Brittany.

Gavin, Gawain, Gawayne ('ga+wane')

These names probably come from

Welsh *gwalch* + *gwyn*, meaning 'white hawk of battle'. Gavin is found in Ireland, Scotland and the Isle of Man. The forms with 'w' were used mainly in Cornwall and Wales.

Geraint, Gereint, Gerent *('ge+raint', 'ge+rent')*

Geraint is now the usual Welsh spelling but the form Gerent is recorded for Cornwall. The story of Gereint and Enid is a popular Arthurian legend. It is likely that all these forms are related to Greek Gerontios, which comes from *geron*, 'old man'. St Gerent was honoured with a church in tenth-century Cornwall and with another in Dol, in Brittany.

Gerwyn *('ger+win')*

This Welsh name looks like Gervin but is unrelated. It means 'fair love'.

Gildas, Gweltaz *('gil+das' and 'gwel+tez')*

Gildas is used in both Wales and Brittany. It is possible that the name comes from French Giles, which was taken from Greek *aigidion*, 'kid'. It has the pet form Gweltaz in Brittany.

Glen, Glenn, Glyn

This comes from Gaelic *gleann*, 'valley', also used also as a surname. Welsh *glyn* also means 'valley' and is mostly used as a first name.

Glendon

Glendon comes from Gaelic *gleann*, 'valley, glen', plus *dún*, fortress, and so implies 'one from the fortress in the glen'.

Gorman, Gormley

Gorman may come from the Gaelic adjective *gorm*, 'blue, noble', and thus Gormley means 'blue-eyed little one' or 'noble warrior'.

Grady

Grady and O'Grady are probably from Gaelic *gradaim*, 'distinction, honour'.

Graham, Grahame, Graeme

Graham is thought of as quintessentially Scottish but the name comes from Old English *grand*, 'gravel', + *ham*, 'settlement'.

Grant

Grant is closely associated with Scotland but it comes from French *grand*, 'big', and was used by the Normans when they settled in Celtic communities.

Gregor

Gregor comes from Gregory, which was originally from Greek *gregorios*, 'watchful'. It is best known in the Scottish clan name MacGregor.

Griffith, Gryffydd
('grif+ith' and 'grif+fidh')

It is not clear where the Welsh name Griffith comes from, although it is suggested that it is a form of *rufus*, meaning 'red-haired'. Rufus is Latin, but it was the nickname of William the Conqueror's son, William Rufus.

Guaire *('gwy+ir+ih')*, Guerar *('gair+are')*, Gwair

These names are probably related, although the first is found in Ireland, the second in Cornwall and the third in Wales. Guaire was a sixth-century Irish king who lived at Gort in Galway. Guerar was a saint buried at St Neot in Cornwall. Gwair is a character in Welsh legends. The meaning is disputed, but Guaire may be related to *gáire* and mean 'laughter, good cheer'.

Gwennin, Gwyn

These names probably both derive

from a Celtic word *gwyn*, 'white, fair, pure'. Gwennin is used in Brittany and Gwyn in Wales.

H

Hamish *('hay+mish')*

Hamish is a Scottish form of Seamus or Seumas. All Celtic names had vocative forms, that is forms used in address. Thus, a boy might be called Seamus, but he would be addressed as '*A Sheamuis*' and this would be pronounced like 'a hyamish'. Hamish is thus a form of James, which means 'heel'.

Harvey, Herve, Herveig *('har+vee', 'air+vay')*

Harvey is thought to be of Breton origin and to mean 'worthy in battle'. The variant Herve is popular again in France.

Hugh, Huw, Kew *('hyoo', 'kyoo')*

The Irish and Scottish Hugh, its Welsh equivalent Huw, and probably the Cornish Kew, are from a Germanic word *hug*, meaning 'heart, mind, spirit' and the same name is found in Hubert, from *hug* + *berht*, 'bright spirit'. The form Hugo is a Latinised form of Hugh.

Hywel *('how+ell')*

Hywel is a Welsh name that means 'eminent'. This name has given rise to the surname Powell, which comes from *ap* + Hywel, 'son of Hywel'. Howell is an anglicised form of Hywel.

I

Ian, Iain, Ieuan, Iwan *('ee+an', 'yew+an')*

Ian and Iain are Scottish forms of John and thus mean 'God is gracious'. They are found in many communities as well as Scotland, while the forms Ieuan and Iwan are found mainly in Wales.

Idris *('ee+driss' or 'eye+driss')*
Idris comes from Welsh *iud*, 'lord' + *ris*, 'fiery, ardent'. It was used in the Middle Ages but then virtually died out, only to be reinstated in the nineteenth and twentieth centuries.

Ifor
Ifor is a Welsh form of the Scandinavian name Ivor, from *yr* + *herr*, 'yew + army', meaning 'archer'.

Inir, Ynyr *('in+eer')*
Inir is a Welsh name, coming from *ynyr*, meaning 'honour'.

Innes, Innis *('in+iss')*
Innis is used as a clan name and a given name in Scotland. The clan name may come from *innis*, 'island'. The given name may also be a form of Aengus.

Iobhar, Ivi *('yo+var', 'ee+vee')*
The Gaelic word *iobhar* or *iúr* means 'yew'. Versions of this name are found in all Celtic languages because it derives from the name of the yew tree. Trees were significant to the Celts and circles of hawthorn, oak or yew trees had mystical significance for the druids. The form Ivi was found in Cornwall and is still used in Brittany, where the feast of Saint Ivi is celebrated on 6 October.

Iollan, Yollan, Yolland *('yoll+an(d)')*
Iollan was the son of Fergal and a champion at the court of Conchubhar. He went from Ireland to Scotland to persuade Deirdre and the sons of Usna to return home as he believed that Conchubhar had forgiven them. When he discovered his mistake, he died defending them. The name may be linked to *íol*, 'one who worships a different god'.

Ithel ('eeth+el')

Ithel seems to come from *ior + hael*, meaning 'generous lord' and is one of many Welsh names currently being used for the first time in centuries.

J

Jago ('jay+go'), Jagu, Jegu, Jacut

Jago is a Cornish form of Jacob, the other three are Breton. Jacob is a Hebrew name which was also anglicised as James. The biblical Jacob was the son of Rebecca and Isaac and the twin brother of Esau. He is said to have held on to his brother's heel when he was born, and so the name may mean 'heel' or it may mean 'supplanter' because Jacob supplanted his brother as Isaac's heir.

Jared, Jarret ('jar+red', 'ja+ret')

Jared and Jar(r)et are related to Gareth and Garrett and come from Germanic, *gar + hard*, which means 'hardy spear (carrier)'. They are used especially in Ireland, where they may have been influenced by the name of a sixth-century saint, Iarlath or Jarlath.

Job, Jos

Job and Jos are used in Brittany as forms of Joseph, a name that means 'God shall add'.

K

Ka, Kai, Kay, Key ('key')

It is possible that this name comes from Gaelic *caoi*, meaning 'path, way', but it is more likely that it comes from Welsh and means 'field of battle'. This was the name of one of King Arthur's knights.

Kane, Kain

Kane may come from *cian*, 'dark one' or from the old Irish name Cathán, meaning 'war champion'.

Keegan

This name comes from a wrong division of MacEgan, becoming MaKeegan and eventually Keegan. It means 'son of the little fire'.

Keelan

Keelan, which comes from *caoil* + *finn* or *fionn* and means 'slender and fair', and could be used equally for boys and girls.

Keir

Keir is a Scottish surname that was popularised as a first name by the politician, Keir Hardie. The name probably comes from *ciar*, meaning 'dark haired'.

Keith

Keith was originally Scottish and probably came from a form of *coillte* or *ceiteach*, meaning 'woods'. It has moved far from Scotland and is now used worldwide. It is possible that Keith was influenced also by Welsh *coedwig*, 'forest', and by Old English *cuth*, 'knowledgeable'.

Kelvin

Kelvin is a Scottish name derived from the River Clyde, and Glasgow has an area, Kelvinside, named after it. The name has been influenced by Melvin.

Kendrick

Kendrick, like many old names, has at least two possible derivations. It may come from the wrong division of Scottish MacEanruigh, 'son of Henry', 'son of home power', or it may come from Old English words meaning 'keen power'. The fact that the name occurs much more widely in Scotland than elsewhere suggests that the Gaelic meaning may be the older one.

Kennedy

This surname originated in Ireland and Scotland and probably comes from *ceann éitigh*, 'ugly head', although some Kennedys suggest that it really means 'helmeted head'. The use of Kennedy as a first name owes much to the respect that was felt for John F. Kennedy, the assassinated President of the United States.

Kenneth

Kenneth almost certainly comes from Scots Gaelic *coinneach*, 'born of fire'. One of the earliest Kenneths was a sixth-century Irish saint who left his monastery after it was ravaged by plague. He spent time in both Wales and Scotland and many legends grew up around him.

Kent

Kent comes from the name of an English county, but the name of the county is almost certainly from an old Celtic word meaning 'border' and is possibly related to Welsh *cenedl*, 'nation'.

Kevin, Caoimhghín, Caoimhín *('cave+een', 'keev+een')*, Cavin, Kevan, Keverne

This name comes from *caomh*, 'beautiful, gentle', and means 'beautiful at birth' or 'handsomely born'. St Kevin was a seventh-century monk who lived at Glendalough and was renowned throughout the Celtic world. The forms Coemgen, Gavin and Kevin are found in Brittany; at least one parish was dedicated to St Keverne in Cornwall; and Kevin is favoured in Scotland, Wales and the Isle of Man.

Kyle

Kyle, which may come from *cill,* 'church', is most frequently used in Scotland, where it is taken from the region that is now in Strathclyde.

Labhras (*'lau+russ', 'low+russ'*)

Labhras is an Irish form of Laurence, based on a Roman place name, Laurentum, although probably influenced by *laurus*, 'laurel wreath', a symbol of high success. There have been several saints called Laurence, the best-known being the third-century martyr.

Lach (*'loch'*), Lachlan, Lachlann, Lochlann
(*'loch+lan'*)

Lachlann is used almost exclusively in Scotland. It means 'Viking, stranger from the land of the lochs'. It sometimes occurs in the surname Loughlan or Loughlin.

Lance, Lancelot, Launcelot

Lancelot's name is one of the best known in Celtic legends. It is not certain what the name means. It has been suggested that it comes from French *lance* and means 'spear carrier', but it is more likely that it was originally a Celtic name connected with *llan*, 'church'.

Lee, Leigh

Lee may have several origins. It may come from Old English *leah*, 'wood'; it may come from Welsh *lle*, 'place'; it may come from the River Lee in Ireland; or from Gaelic *laoi*, 'poem, lay'.

Lennon

Lennon is a popular Irish surname, possibly from *léana* meaning 'meadow'. It started being used as a first name after the death of the Beatle John Lennon in 1980.

Lennox

Lennox is a surname in Scotland. It was originally a placename and probably came from *leamhán*, 'elm' and meant 'grove of elms'.

Liam

Liam is the Irish form of William, originally a Germanic name, *wil(l)* + *helm*, meaning 'will + helmet' and probably suggesting 'strong protection'. The Normans took the name to England in 1066 in the form of Guillaume, and Liam is probably an Irish version of this, rather than the second half of William.

Llewellyn, Llywelyn

(*'hloo+ell+in'*), **Llew**

Llewellyn is the slightly anglicised form of a Welsh name, Llywelyn, that was borne by a Welsh prince, Llywelyn ap Iorweth, in the twelfth century. Its meaning is uncertain but it is claimed to include *llew*, 'lion', and mean 'lionlike, mighty ruler'.

Lloyd (*'hloid' or 'loid'*)

Lloyd comes from the Welsh adjective *llwyd*, meaning 'grey' and suggesting 'grey-haired, mature'. It has also been anglicised as Floyd, because English speakers found it hard to begin a name with the Welsh sound represented by 'll'.

Loeiz, Loic, Loig

(*'loo+eece' or 'loo+eek'*)

These are Breton forms of Louis, a name that was originally Germanic *hlod* + *wig*, 'fame + war', and meant 'famous in war'. It was the most frequently used king's name in France from the Middle Ages until the French Revolution.

Logan

Logan is a surname in Scotland and Ireland and probably comes from *logán*, meaning 'hollow'.

Lorcan, Lorcán

The Gaelic word *lorc* means 'fierce' and the name was probably a nickname for a brave warrior. It is sometimes equated with Laurence, but is a name in its own right.

Lugh *('Lou')*

Lugh is related to Gaelic *luisne*, 'glow of light' and means 'shining light'. He was, as we might expect, a god and thus qualified to perform any task.

Lughaidh *('loo+ee')*

Lughaidh's name is based on Lugh and thus probably means 'carrier of light'. Lughaidh has the dubious fame of having defeated Cúchulainn in single combat. However, even the sword he used to behead the great warrior objected and cut off Lughaidh's own hand.

M

Macaulay, Macauley

Macaulay comes from Irish *mac + amhlach*, 'son of the phantom'.

Mackenzie, Mack

Mackenzie has become popular as a first name in Canada and America, largely among people of Scottish origin. The name means 'son of the bright one' and the Mackenzies have been a significant clan in Scotland for at least 700 years.

Madeg, Madoc, Madog *('ma+deg', 'ma+dock')*

Madeg and Madoc are Breton forms of the Welsh name Madoc, meaning 'generous, forgiving'. They are also probably related to Malachy, which may come from *mael + Madog*, 'follower of St Madog', a seventh-century Irish monk revered throughout the Celtic and Christian world.

Mael, Malo, Mel

Mael, probably meaning 'devotee', is found in Brittany and has a feminine form Maela.

Maeldún, Maelduine, Muldoon *('mwel+doon', 'mel+doon', 'mull+doon')*

Maeldún is an Irish traveller in the

mould of St Brendan. His name may mean 'devotee of the dark warrior' or *dún* may refer to 'fortress'.

Malachy *('mal+a+kee')*

Malachy comes from the Irish name *maoilsheachlainn*, and means 'follower or devotee of St Seachlainn'. It was equated with the Hebrew prophet Malachi, whose name means 'messenger of God'.

Malcolm

Malcolm is one of the most popular Gaelic names. It comes from Gaelic *maol* (*mael*) + *colm* and means 'follower or devotee of the dove', where the 'dove' is usually St Columba.

Mangan

The Gaelic adjective *mongach* means 'with plenty of hair' and this nickname has become both a given name and a surname.

Manus

Manus, or less frequently Magnus, is used as a first name in Ireland. It comes originally from Latin *magnus*, 'big, great', and was popularised by Charlemagne, or Carolus Magnus, Charles the Great, crowned Roman Emperor in AD 800.

Maolíosa *('mwell+ee+sa')*

This name has become popular for both boys and girls. It is from *maol* + *Íosa*, meaning 'devotee of Jesus'.

Marvin, Mervin, Morvan

Marvin comes from Welsh *myrddyn*, meaning 'sea fort'. It is the same name as both Merlin and Mervin and all of them are anglicisations. The form Morvan is found in Brittany. This could also be seen as a blend of Mervin and Morgan.

Melor, Melorus, Mylor

Melor was probably a Breton saint,

who continues to be honoured in Brittany, but some traditions suggest that he was the son of a Cornish king and a Devonian lady. He was patron saint of Mylor in Cornwall. His name may mean 'iron man', the same as Welsh *meilyr*, or the '*mel-*' may suggest that he was a new devotee of a particular saint, since *úr* means 'new'.

Melville, Melvin, Melvyn

These names are all derived from a Scottish placename, Malleville, settled by the Normans and named 'bad town', presumably because the land was infertile. Malleville became Melville. The change from Melville to Melvin was helped by the existence of other names ending in '-in'. The '-yn' spelling was the result of fashion.

Merlin, Merlyn

Merlin is the sorceror of King Arthur and the Knights of the Round Table. His name comes from Welsh *myrddyn*, meaning 'sea fort', a name that has also been anglicised as Marvin and Mervin.

Merven, Mervin, Mervyn

It seems likely that Mervyn and its variants come from Welsh *merfyn*, supposedly from *mer*, 'marrow' + *ffynu*, 'thriving'. Certainly, it was the name of a ninth-century Welsh king. Alternative origins suggest that Mervyn and Melvin are variants of Malvin and refer to a devotee of Mena, or of Merlin.

Micheál *('me+hall')*, Mikael, Mitchell

Micheál is an Irish form of Michael, a Hebrew name, meaning 'who is like God', and borne by the Archangel who cast Lucifer into Hell. He was often depicted as a soldier, bearing a sword of flame.

The abbreviations Mick, Mickey, Mike and Mikey are also used in Ireland. The form Mikael is Breton. Mitchell is a variant of Michael, and Mitch an abbreviation.

Milo *('mile+o')*

It is possible that this name comes from Latin *milo*, a miller, or is an Irish form of Miles/Myles, or that it is a shortened form of *maol + Muire*, meaning 'devotee of Mary'.

Morgan

Morgan can be linked to both Irish and Welsh and may mean either 'great queen' or 'bright sea, sea born'. The modern Irish word *móraigeanta*, 'magnanimous', is related.

Muireachadh

('moor+a+hoo'), **Murdo, Murrough, Murphy**

Murdo is a form of the Gaelic name Muireachadh, meaning 'man/hound of the sea', that has also given rise to Murdoch, Murray and possibly Murphy. Murphy is an Irish surname that comes from *muir + cath*, 'sea + battle', and probably implying 'warrior from the sea'. It was originally a nickname, then a first name, a surname, and now a given name again.

Munro

Munro, like a lot of Celtic names, carries in it a history of people and places. The name originated in Ireland as *bun*, 'mouth of' + *Roe*, a river, possibly meaning 'red'. The 'b' in Gaelic can become 'm' in certain circumstances. The place-name was anglicised as Munro or Monroe and used as a surname. The surname was taken to Scotland, where it began to be used as a first name, usually ending in '-o'.

Murray

Murray can be an anglicised form

of Muireachadh, but it can also come from Moray, in Scotland. Murray is used quite often as a first name in Scotland, and occasionally in Northern Ireland, where Moray also occurs.

Murtagh *('mer + tah')*

Murtagh is an old Gaelic name probably from *muirchath* meaning 'sea-battle' and although its popularity waned for many centuries, it is again being used, sometimes in the Irish form and sometimes in the Scottish form, Murdoch.

N

Naoise, Naoisi *('nee+shih')*, **Nyse**

Naoise was the lover of Deirdre. Its meaning is uncertain although it may be associated with *nasc*, 'bond'. Traditionally, the name Naoise has been regarded as the Irish equivalent of Noah, meaning 'rest'.

Neal, Neil, Niall *(sometimes pronounced to rhyme with 'feel' and sometimes as 'nigh+ell')*, Nigel

Neal and Neil are used both as given names and as surnames. They come from Niall, which is an older version and probably comes from Irish *niadh*, 'champion'. A famous king of Tara was Niall of the Nine Hostages; no-one is certain how his name arose. Nigel comes from Nigellus, a medieval Latin form of Niall.

Nedeleg, Nodhlag, Nodhlaig, Noel, Nollaig

These names mean Christmas and are thus the equivalent of Noel. They are often given to boys born on 25 December. Nedeleg is the Breton form and the other variants are found in Ireland.

Nelson

Nelson is a blend of Niall, 'champion', and 'son'. It was given a boost as a first name in the nineteenth century after Admiral Nelson's victory at Trafalgar.

Nevan, Neven, Nevin, Niven, Nivin

Nevan is related to *naomh*, 'saint, holy one' and was originally a nickname given to a religious person. Various forms of the name occur in Scotland, especially as surnames and may come from Norman French and be related to 'nephew'.

Nuada *('noo+ah+da')*

Nuada was a king of the Tuatha de Danaan, the gods of ancient Ireland. His name may be related to modern Irish *nua dhéanta*, 'newly made'.

Odhrán, Odran, Oran, Oren, Orin, Orna, Orren, Orrin *('o+ran' or 'or+na')*

Oran probably comes from *odhra*, meaning 'dark-haired'. St Oran was Irish but spent much of his life spreading Christianity in Scotland. Most of the saints of this name were male but the name seems to be preferred for girls.

Oisín, Ossian *('osh+een', 'oss+ee+an')*

Oisín was the son of Fionn Mac-Cool, the leader of the Fianna, and of Saeve or Sive, a goddess. Sive was turned into a deer before her son was born and she brought him up in the forest, giving him the name *oisín*, that means 'little deer'. When Fionn was hunting, he found the child and recognised him as his son. Ossian is the form of Oisín used by the Scottish poet,

James Macpherson, who published *The Poems of Ossian* in 1765.

Oscar, Osgar, Osgur

Oscar is usually described as a Scandinavian name deriving from *os* + *gar*, meaning 'god's spear'. However, Oscar was the name of Oisín's son and means 'lover of deer' or 'beloved of deer'; the Gaelic word for 'deer' is *os*.

Owain, Owen, Eoghan, Eoin, Euan, Evan, Ewen

These names are variants of a Celtic name meaning 'well born' or 'yew born'. It is popular in different forms in the different Celtic communities. The Welsh Owain fought against the Angles, the Germanic people who gave their name to England ('Engla + land') and Owain (or Owen) Glyndwr led an uprising against King Henry IV in the fifteenth century.

Ownie, Owny, Uaine, Uaithne

In Ireland, the popular name Ownie or Owny is usually regarded as a diminutive form of 'Owen', but it is a name in its own right and is related to *uaine*, 'green, verdant' and the phrase *uaine gháire* means 'a peal of laughter'.

P

Paddy, Páid ('paw+id', 'paw+idge'), Páidín ('paw+idge+een'), Pat, Patsy, Rick

These are abbreviated forms of Padraig and Patrick, both forms of *patricius*, 'of noble birth'.

Padraic, Pádraic ('paw+drick'), Padraig ('paw+drig'), Padrig, Padruig, Patric, Patrice, Patrick

These names are all derived from

the Latin *patricius*, 'nobly born, Patrician' although it is possible that this was a nickname and that the patron saint of Ireland had a Celtic name. There are so many legends and traditions about St Patrick that it is virtually impossible to be certain about anything. What is probably true is that he was born in Britain around AD 373 and spoke a Celtic language, but we cannot be sure which one. He was captured as a youth by Irish raiders and forced to guard sheep. He escaped and trained as a priest on the Continent and eventually, after several visions, made his way back to Ireland, where he converted the population to Christianity. Patrick's fame spread far beyond the Celtic regions, and versions of the name Patrick are found and used in virtually all countries.

Peada(i)r *('padh+er')*

Peadar is an Irish form of Peter

and thus comes ultimately from Greek *petros*, 'rock'.

Pearce, Pearse, Per, Perig, Piaras, Pierce, Piers

The Normans used Piers as a form of Latin Petrus, which came ultimately from Greek *petros*, 'rock'. The Irish borrowed this as Pearce, Piaras, Pierce and, less frequently, Piers. The name was so popular that it was adopted also as a surname. The forms Per and Perig continue to be popular in Brittany.

Pedr

This is a Welsh form of Peter. It would have appealed to Welsh speakers because of its similarity to Peredur.

Petroc *('pet+rock')*, Petrog, Petroke

These names seem to be Celtic forms of the Greek *petros*, 'rock'. In the sixth century, Petroc founded a monastery in Padstow, Cornwall. He was renowned for his love of animals and his ability to communicate with them.

Phelan ('fail+an', 'feel+an'), Faolán ('fwail+awn'), Felan

Phelan is an anglicised spelling of Faolán or Felan, a name that comes from a literary word *faol*, meaning 'wolf'. The earliest record of the name seems to be for a follower of Fionn who was so loyal that nothing could keep him from his lord.

Phelim ('fail+im', 'feel+im'), Phelimy, Feidhlim, Felim, Feidhlimidh ('fail+im+ee'), Felimy

Phelim is an anglicised form of Feidhlim, a name that comes from *feidhil*, meaning 'constant, always enduring'. The name has been held by king, poet and warrior.

Pól ('pole')

The name of St Paul was borrowed into the Celtic languages as Paulus, which comes from Latin *paulus* and means 'little one'. The form Pól is a modern borrowing. The pronunciation suggests that it was borrowed from French, rather than from English Paul.

Powell ('pow+ill')

Powell is a form of *ap* + Hywel, 'son of Hywel'. Its popularity may have been enhanced by the existence of Pwyll, meaning 'prudence'.

Proinsias ('pron+shee+iss')

Proinsias is an Irish form of Francis. The name, which means 'French man', was popularised in Ireland by the Franciscans, whose founder was St Francis of Assisi.

Pryce ('price')

This Welsh name is a form of *ap* + Rhys, 'son of Rhys'.

Pwyll ('pow+ill')

Pwyll is a Welsh name meaning 'prudence'. The legendary Pwyll was the lord of Dyfed and the husband of Rhiannon, to whom he was utterly devoted. He was also renowned for his great courtesy, a virtue highly regarded by the Celts.

Q

Quinn

Quinn is probably a variant of the name Conn, meaning 'intelligent'. It is an extremely common surname in Northern Ireland, a fact that may have given rise to its use as a given name.

R

Raghallaigh ('rah+hal+ee'), Reilly, Riley ('rye+lee')

These are all forms of a Gaelic adjective *raghalach*, probably meaning 'courageous, valiant'. The name has begun to be used as a first name although it is still mostly a surname in Ireland and other places where the Irish have settled.

Re(a)gan ('ray+gan', 'ree+gan')

The meaning of Re(a)gan, like the pronunciation, is not fixed. It is likely that it is related to the Gaelic *rí* and thus means 'like a king', or it may come from *ríogach* and mean 'impulsive'. Like a lot of Irish names, it started as a nickname, became a first name, then a surname and is now used again as a given name.

Réaman(n), Reamon ('ray+mon'), Redmond

These are all Irish versions of the Germanic name *rad + mund*, meaning 'counsellor and protector'. The name was particularly popular in Northern Ireland, where the seventeenth-century Redmond O'Hanlon was a renowned highwayman.

Reece, Rees *('hrees', 'rees')*, Rhett, Rhys

These names seem to be derived from Welsh *rhys* and to mean 'ardour, passion'. The first two forms are anglicisations of Rhys and Rhett is probably a pet form of the name. Rhett Butler was the hero in *Gone With The Wind*.

Rhain *('hra+in')*

This name is sometimes confused with Ryan but, although they are both Celtic, they are not related. Rhain is Welsh and means 'lance', a name that implied 'brave warrior'.

Rhodri

There was a ninth-century Welsh ruler called Rhodri. It is probable that the name is related to *rhod*, 'wheel', although it may have been influenced by *rhoddwr*, 'bestower of gifts'.

Riobard *(rib+awrd)*, Riobart, Roibeard, Roibeart, Rab, Rob

These are versions of Robert, which is not a Celtic name but was taken to Celtic areas by the Normans. It comes from *hrod + berht*, meaning 'bright fame'. The Scots adopted it as Rab and Rabbie, and their national poet is usually referred to as Rabbie Burns.

Roarke, Rorke, Rourke, Ruark *('row+erk', 'roo+erk')*

These are all variants of an Irish name meaning 'famous ruler'.

Roc, Rock

Roc was a follower of Aengus Óg. His son was killed by an angry man but Roc was able to transform the dead son into a living boar, an animal sacred to the Celts. The meaning of Roc is unclear. It may be related to the Irish *rocaí*, 'person with frizzy hair'. It can be spelt with a 'k' and has Rocky as a diminutive form.

Roddy, Roden, Rody

The Irish adjective *ród* means 'strong' and has given rise to the name Roden or Rodin, meaning 'the strong one'. This name helps to explain the popularity of Roderick, especially in its abbreviated form of Rod(d)y.

Rogan

Rogan is one of the many Celtic names from the Gaelic *ruadh*, meaning 'red-haired'. There are many '-*ogan*' surnames in Ireland: Brogan, Hogan, Logan, Rogan and Wogan, and all but Wogan occur as given names. Rogan is extremely popular worldwide and is found in Zambia and Zimbabwe as well as Europe, America and Australia.

Ronan *('ro+nan')*

Ronan comes from *rón* and means 'little seal'. It is found as a first name in Brittany, Ireland, the Isle of Man and Scotland. According to Celtic tradition, sea women could put on and take off the form of a seal and could, in certain circumstances, live with a human man. Their children would be 'ronans' or 'little seals'.

Rory, Ruadhrí, Ruarí

('ro+ree', 'roo+ir+ee')

Rory is popular in Ireland and Scotland, and indeed throughout the English-using world. It may come from Gaelic *ruadh* and mean 'redhead' or from *ruadh + rí* and mean 'red + king'. It is sometimes used as a diminutive form of Roderick, although the two names are unconnected.

Ross

This name almost certainly comes from Gaelic *ros* meaning 'headland' and found in such Irish places as The Rosses in Donegal or Roscommon, or in Scottish place-names such as Rostrevor. Ross is both a surname and a first name and has been used as a given name since the days of Fionn MacCool when Ros was a warrior and a contemporary of Cúchulainn.

Rowan, Ruad(h)an
('roo+awn')

Rowan has two main pronunciations: the first syllable may rhyme with 'hoe' or with 'how'. It seems to be a variant of Gaelic *ruad(h) an* and meant 'little redhead'. It is the name of a number of saints, and since the time of the Vikings it has been equated with the rowan tree, a tree with bright red berries and sometimes associated with the tree on which Christ was crucified. Ruad(h)an appears in Gaelic mythology as the son of Brigit and Bres and a warrior of great skill and courage.

Roy

Roy almost certainly started in Scotland as a nickname from *ruadh*, meaning 'red', as in Sir Walter Scott's *Rob Roy*. However, it is often thought to come from French *roi*, meaning 'king', and both these meanings cling to the name. Roy was very popular in the 1940s when Roy Rogers was the most popular Hollywood cowboy.

Rumo, Rumon

Although Rumo or Rumon is regarded as a Cornish saint, whose name seems to be associated with 'red', it is possible that he came from Brittany and may even be one of the saints called Ronan. According to Cornish tradition, Rumo was a bishop who was martyred for his faith.

Ryan

No-one is absolutely certain what Ryan means, although the first syllable probably comes from Gaelic *rí*, meaning 'king'. It is possible that it means 'little king' or 'royalty'.

S

Sayer

Sayer is a surname that means 'carpenter, craftsman'. It comes from Gaelic *saor*; the phrase *An Saor* is used for God and often translated as 'the Great Architect'. The word *saor* also means 'free', and the anglicised form Sayer began to be used at the time of Irish independence.

Scott

Scott is, of course, a variant spelling for Scot, meaning both 'painted warrior' and 'person from Scotland'. The clan known as Scotii actually moved to Scotland from Ireland in the sixth century.

Seamus, Seumas, Seumus, Hamish

Seamus is one of the best-known and most widely-used Irish names and yet it is a form of James, meaning 'supplanter'. The forms Seumas and Hamish are found mainly in Scotland. Although Seamus cannot claim to be a Celtic name in origin, there is an ancient Irish name Semias that may have encouraged the popularity of Seamus.

Seán, Sean, Shane, Shaughan, Shaun, Shawn

These are all forms of the Irish version of John, meaning 'God is gracious' or 'God's gracious gift'. The two main pronunciations, rhyming with 'dawn' and 'Dane', reflect the pronunciations favoured in the south and north of Ireland, respectively. There is a third pronunciation rhyming with 'Dan' but this is less widespread.

Seanán, Senan, Sezni, Shannon, Sionán, Zenan

These variants are all related to *sean*, 'old' and all mean 'old, wise'. There was a sixth-century Irish saint called Senan, who was renowned throughout the Celtic world and who may be the source of Breton Sezni and Cornish Zenan. The Cornish also had a female saint, 'Sancta Senan' or 'Sancta Senara' but little is known about her. The name could apply equally to a man or a woman because it was really a term of respect, like 'senator'.

Seosamh ('sho+soo', 'sho+siv')

Seosamh is the Irish form of Joseph, a Hebrew name meaning 'God shall add'. Joseph was the husband of the Blessed Virgin Mary.

Setanta

Setanta was the original name of Cúchulainn.

Shea ('shay')

Shea comes from an old Irish given name, Sé, meaning 'like a hawk' and implying 'graceful, keen-sighted, courageous, strong, free'.

Sheridan

Sheridan is an Irish surname that has begun to be used as a given name. Its meaning is uncertain although it may include *síor*, meaning 'eternal', and *dán*, meaning 'treasure, poem'.

Sinclair

Sinclair is so widely regarded as a Scottish name that it is not always realised that it comes from 'Saint Claire' and thus means 'holy light'. The Scottish Sinclairs came from St Claire-sur-Elle in Normandy.

Stewart, Stuart

The origin of these names goes back to the Middle Ages, when Sir Walter Fitz-Allan was made the High Steward of Scotland by King David I. Fourteen Stewarts or Stuarts have ruled, either in Scotland or in England. One of the best-known was Mary Stuart, Queen of Scots, executed by Elizabeth I.

Sulian, Sulien
('soo+lee+en')

Sulian is occasionally used in Brittany as a form of Julian, a name that comes from Latin Julius. The name Sulien is occasionally used for Julian, but comes from Welsh and is said to mean 'sun-born' or 'summer baby'.

T

Tadhg *(like first syllable in 'tiger')*

Tadhg is an Irish name meaning 'poet'. It is sometimes pro-

nounced 'tad' in America and written as Tadd or, occasionally, Todd, although these are unrelated names, the first meaning 'father' and the second 'fox'. Many Irish people translate Tadhg as Tim, thus equating it with Timothy, meaning 'God's honour'.

Teilo

Teilo was an early Welsh saint who was renowned for his piety and his preaching. It is not easy to say what Teilo's name means but it could be related to *teilwng*, 'worthy'.

Ter(r)ence, Torrance

Ter(r)ence is a popular Irish name, derived from Latin *terentius* and probably meaning 'polished'. The name Torrance occurs in Ireland and is possibly a blend of Torin and Ter(r)ence.

Tiernan ('tee+ir+nan'), Tierney

Both these names come from *tighern*, 'lord', and Tiernan is often translated as 'lord of the household, chief'.

Tomás ('tom+moss')

Tomás is the Irish form of Thomas, a biblical name meaning 'twin'.

Torin

Torin is often thought to be an anglicisation of Gaelic *torfhinn*, meaning 'chief' or *tóirneach*, meaning 'thunder', and the link with Thor, the Viking god of thunder, is clear. The name is also found in Cornwall and the Isle of Man.

Tostig ('toss+tig', 'tuss+tig')

This Welsh name means 'pointed' and suggests 'warrior'.

Trefor, Trevor

Like many Celtic names, this one has been used as a placename, a surname and now, almost exclusively, as a given name. It comes from Welsh *tref* + *for*, meaning 'large settlement'. Irrespective of spelling, the Welsh tend to pronounce the name with a central '-f-' but others prefer the '-v-' pronunciation. The word *tref* originally meant 'farmstead' and is related to the Gaelic *treabhadh*, 'ploughing'.

Tristan, Tristram

Tristan's name occurs in various forms but it is likely that they have all been influenced by French *triste*, 'sad'.

Turloch, Turlough ('ter+loch', 'toor+loch'), Turlow

Turlough is an Irish name possibly meaning 'initiator' or 'shaped like Thor', the Viking god of thunder.

Tyrone *('tir+own' in Ireland and 'tie+rone' elsewhere)*

Tyrone is the name of a county in Northern Ireland. It means 'land of Eoghan, land of the noble'.

U

Ultán *('ool+tawn')*

Ultán means 'Ulsterman' and it is the name of several of the many saints from Ulster. A famous seventh-century St Ultán went to France and was renowned throughout Europe for his piety and simplicity.

V,

Vaughan *('vawn')*, Vychan

Vaughan derives from the Welsh adjective *bychan*, meaning 'small'.

W

Wallace, Walsh, Wallis, Welch, Welsh

Wallace and its various forms comes from an Anglo-Saxon word

wealh, meaning 'foreigner'. The Latin equivalent Wallensis was used in Scotland to describe the Celts, especially those who lived in the Strathclyde area.

Y

Yann

This form of John was found in both Breton and Cornish. It means 'God is gracious' and was once one of the most popular Celtic names.

Yestin *('yes+tin')*

Yestin is used in Welsh as the equivalent of Justin, meaning 'fair, just'. St Justin was a second-century theologian.

Ynyr *('in+ir')*

Ynyr is a Welsh form of Latin Honorius, meaning 'honour'.